Muscle

Carlton Leach

D0273560

Published by John Blake Publishing Ltd,
3 Bramber Court, 2 Bramber Road, London W14 9PB, England

This edition first published in 2003

ISBN 1 904034 48 9

British Library Cataloguing-in-Publication Data:
A catalogue record for this book is available from
the British Library.

Design by ENVY

Printed and bound in Great Britain by Bookmarque

7 9 10 8 6

Papers used by John Blake Publishing Ltd are natural, recyclable products
made from wood grown in sustainable forests. The manufacturing processes conform
to the environmental regulations of the country of origin.

Every attempt has been made to contact the relevant copyright-holders, but some
were untraceable. We would be grateful if the appropriate people could contact us.

**'The most dangerous people
I ever met were my friends.'**

CARLTON LEACH

Contents

	PREFACE	VII
1	'ROID RAGE	1
2	CARNAGE	33
3	GHOSTS	53
4	DOOR WARS	67
5	BAD VIBRATIONS	85
6	KING OF THE HOOLIGANS	103
7	DUTCH COURAGE	123
8	SORTED	135
9	VIVA ESPAÑA	149
10	CHEQUE MATE	159
11	THE BENN YEARS	179
12	MOLLS	195
13	TALKING TURKEY	211
14	WELCOME HOME, SON	231
15	RAVING MAD	251
16	FOUR MURDERS AND A FUNERAL	269

Preface

For 20 years, Carlton Leach ranked among the toughest of Britain's brawn brigade. He led a powerful army of bruisers involved in the lucrative world of security and protection, from club doormen at top nightspots to underworld minders guarding millions of pounds of drug-trafficking cash.

He was a key member of the dreaded Essex Boys gang which ran riot in the Eighties and Nineties, sparking a savage drugs war which saw three of his pals wiped out in the 1995 Range Rover massacre at Rettendon. He gives a unique insight into the ruthless world of modern-day gangland and believes his name is on a bullet to become yet another casualty of that simmering feud.

His notoriety made him a star of a TV documentary on Britain's worst soccer thugs. He featured in Channel 5's hit series *Hard Bastards* with the chilling words, 'In my game, the choice is jail or a grave.'

Leach, now 42, was minder to boxing champ Nigel Benn throughout his glory years in the ring and tells the blood, sweat and tears inside story of their special relationship.

Once a 17-stone man-mountain buoyed up on massive doses of steroids, he recounts the day he defied a crazed gunman's bullets at a London rave party, then saw the man left for dead in an alley as his heavy mob exacted instant justice, underworld style.

And he tells how he saved four of his firm from being tortured to death and their wives and daughters raped in front of them after a £10 million consignment of heroin went missing.

He has been questioned by police in connection with four murders but says he never killed anyone, 'although it came pretty close to it a few times'.

Leach still earns a living from his muscle as one of the most successful debt collectors in the country.

He lives by a primitive code of conduct, whereby only the toughest and most ruthless survive. Image, reputation and respect are all important. But scratch beneath the surface and the human face of Carlton Leach emerges, a father dedicated to his children – especially the son he gave up for adoption at birth and met again 25 years later – a generous man who would be rich today if he hadn't given most of his money away to friends in need, a compassionate man who cried unashamedly when his pet dog died.

To those in his world he was a fearless ally, but a deadly

enemy prepared to use guns, knives and coshes to defend his territory. To those outside his world, he appears a brutal monster who has used violence and intimidation as a frightening form of currency throughout his adult life with the sole aim of making easy money. He is, in fact, a complex combination of good and bad, as he readily admits, and leaves it to the reader to conclude where the scales of justice will rest on judgement day.

Like so many truly hard men, he is adored by wives and girlfriends past and present and idolised by his four children.

This is Carlton Leach, muscle for hire.

Mike Fielder
January, 2002

1

'Roid Rage

The first thing that caught my eye was that the geezer had a gold tooth.

The second was that he was holding a shooter.

And the third that he was pointing it at me.

My door work and bodyguard work had taken me deep into gangland, into the dangerous world of the blaggers and the drug-dealers, turf wars and terminations. Now someone was coming to terminate me. With violence all around me for the last 20 years and my battle scars evident for all to see, I was now facing the possibility of an early epitaph on my tombstone.

Strangely enough, at that moment in time, as dawn slowly lit up London and I stood facing the gunman beside the River Thames at Battersea, I didn't particularly care. I was fuelled up on steroids and speed, a 17-stone man-mountain, and I was feeling no pain. The drugs had made me feel invincible. The geezer with the .45 was not a threat, he was a challenge.

I found myself shouting at him, 'Come on then, you cunt, shoot me.' My safety mechanism had snapped. That little man in my head who comes along when I'm in deep shit and says, 'Don't do it ... don't be silly now, Carlton,' had taken a hike. There was just this lunatic standing there, full of bravado, full of drugs, caution thrown to the wind, saying, 'Come on then, kill me.'

The black geezer was getting closer, his eyes were wide and glazed, his face was a twisted smile, the gun hand unsteady. He was obviously out of it, probably crack. The smile wasn't because he was pleased to see me. We'd clashed earlier and he was back for revenge.

Me and big Chris and a few other lumps were doing the door at a special boat party, members only, which had been laid on by some of the rave crowd. These two black guys had turned up and walked up the gangplank towards the boat. I told them it was invitation only. I could see some of the girls at the party looked scared. These two blokes had given them trouble earlier. I tried to be diplomatic.

'Look, mate, it's membership only and we've got our capacity on board.'

The biggest of them muttered something like, 'I'm so and so, I go where I want.'

I said, 'I don't give a fuck who you are. You're not welcome.'

A fight kicked off and I grabbed him by the throat, pulled out a knife and said, 'Look, mate, we don't want this grief. You've caused the fucking problem. If you don't fuck off I'm going to drag you behind that tree and cut your fucking throat. How do you want it?'

All the boys were on steroids those days and were pumped up and growling at everybody like wild animals. Not a pretty sight. Off the black guys went muttering dire threats that they'd be back to kill us. We were told they'd been trying to get on to the boat parties for a couple of weeks but kept getting turned away. One was a crack-dealer and a heavy cocaine user. Dangerous people and not to be underestimated.

We thought they'd got the message from the assembled heavies blocking their path and wouldn't give any more hassle. How wrong can you be? Half-an-hour later, they were back. By now, I knew the main man was called Mr L. I discovered he had a track record for violence and brutality and headed one of the biggest dealer rings in South London. He was back for vengeance. He stood there for a few seconds smiling at me. Then he unzipped his leather jacket. Before he could pull out a weapon, we were on him. Bang, bang, bang. He was on the floor.

I said, 'We've warned you, we know who you are, we know how bad you are, so if you come back again we'll have to kill you.' With that, I cut him across the face, a fucking great gash down his cheek. He'd pushed and pushed. It was 7.00 in the morning, I'd worked two different clubs through the night and I was at my limit. It had to be settled here and now. As I cut him, I said, 'Right, that's your final warning. Fuck off and keep out of my way or you're dead.'

The combination of tiredness, drugs and raging anger saw me talking like a psychopath. But I really needed this cunt off my back. I hoped he'd got the message. Again, I'd read it wrong.

The sun was fighting its way through heavy cloud over London at the start of a new day, already marred by aggravation. I'd agreed to do the door at the boat party 'til 2.00 in the afternoon, and we were starting to relax. I was sitting on the Thames wall talking, a couple of my boys were sitting in my new BMW 535i having a snort of coke off the back of my *A–Z* when a car pulled up in the street about 100 yards away. I saw a black bloke wearing a baseball cap with a big sticky plaster slapped across his face, almost comical, as though in a cartoon. Andy said, 'It's that black geezer.'

I said, 'No, no it's not, can't be.'

It was; and he was looking for trouble big time now. He walked up the slope towards us. Then he pulled out the shooter. The boys started ducking for cover. As he got nearer, I could see he was still out of it. He was laughing like he was really enjoying the situation. He was getting nearer, the Browning automatic looking bigger and bigger with each stride. The gold tooth was gleaming.

To this day, I don't know what made me do it, but the brave pills kicked in and I was fronting him up and saying, 'Come on, you cunt, shoot me.' Whether this was sheer stupidity or the ultimate test of my fearlessness I don't know. I'd done a lot of things to test my arsehole, but this was pushing it now. That little devil was in my ear saying, 'Do it, do it.'

Now there were about 15 yards between us. 'If you want me, you'll have to kill me,' I taunted him. My sense of self-preservation was gone. I pulled out a knife and shouted, 'Come on then, you want some of this?'

I'm not sure those were the words I really wanted to come out, but the devil was in charge. I was frightened inside. I knew I could die here. But the wrong words kept coming. 'Go on then, you cunt, kill me.'

I wanted the other words in my head – 'Carlton, fuck off out of here' – to prevail, but they didn't. There was a stand-off of a few seconds. It seemed like hours. The gun was waving around a bit in his hand like it was too heavy for him to control. But it was still pointed my way. Then he took a shot at me. Bang!

Now everybody was running and screaming. The bullet whizzed past my left ear and thudded into the wooden hull of the boat. I thought, Fuck, he's really going to kill me. I knew I had to kill him first. The power of the steroids and the coke made me feel strong again. I could walk through a wall. Then, suddenly, I wasn't frightened any more. I was bouncing a bit by now. I yelled, 'Come on then.'

He fired another shot – Bang! That went past the other ear. He was running towards me and the next shot might not miss. I looked for some cover behind a tree.

Bang! He took another shot. Then he clocked my car with two of the doormen in it. He didn't know it was mine but decided to shoot it up anyway. He fired one through the roof and it hit the *A–Z* with the coke on. It missed Paul by an inch. Rather than waste the gear, Paul quickly closed the book around West Kensington and trapped the powder in it.

The gunman put another couple of shots into the car and I was working out how many bullets he'd got left. I knew it could only be a few. Was it a 9mm clip with half-a-dozen or so bullets? Or was it a more modern gun with up to 13 shots? A gamble now could be fatal. If I miscalculated by one single shot, I could become yet another statistic in the underworld's hall of infamy.

Now big Chris was starting to move in on the gunman. The gun was being waved about in all directions. There was no telling where the next shot might go. And if Mr L was looking for a big target, ex-marine Chris could be it – 6ft 4in and 20 stone of well-toned muscle. Chris was working as a fireman and moonlighting as a bouncer so he didn't need any hassle that might get him sacked by the brigade.

As I was thinking he should just fuck off out of it, they were tussling at close range. Then another bang and a wisp of smoke. Chris's bomber jacket puffed out from the blast. I thought, Shit, he's been hit. He slumped to the floor. This could be really bad news. The nutter has wounded him, or worse, killed him stone dead.

I was working my way towards him from the cover of the trees. I was thinking, Got to get to him, got to help him. Me and a couple of others were ready to charge in. Then we realised Chris was playing possum, pretending he was wounded. As the gunman turned away Chris lurched up off the ground and grabbed his arm. The shot had ruffled his coat, ripped through his baggies and just grazed his leg but hadn't caused any serious injury. Relief all round for a few seconds. I ran at them and dived over the car bonnet. Me and Chris wrestled him to the ground. Someone emptied the gun. Then we dragged him down an alleyway nearby and he knew what revenge was all about. He received a savage beating, more than 20 stab wounds, and was as close to death as it's possible to be while still breathing. In fact, we thought he was dead.

We could hear the sound of police sirens and a Scotland Yard helicopter. We quickly grabbed up the tools that had been used – knives, coshes and knuckledusters – and threw them into the Thames. The tide was out and we saw them sink into the mud, hopefully hidden for ever from the Yard's finest. We went on to the boat and cleaned ourselves up as the police arrived in force with machine-guns and flak jackets. Then we had to get Chris off the plot because of his job. We had to get Paul away because he was on curfew and shouldn't have been there. I couldn't go anywhere anyway because my car was so badly shot up, so I said I'd stay behind with one other doorman and talk to the Old Bill, or tell them as much as they needed to know. I'd got about £2,000 in door takings in my shot-up motor and I needed to get that out of the way.

The police said, 'Is this your car?'

I said, 'Er, yes,' and saw the *A–Z* on the back seat with some Charlie still on it. There's a big fucker with a machine-gun standing right beside me so, without really thinking, I picked up the book and snorted the gear up my nostrils before the cops had a chance to twig what was happening.

That was all I needed, Old Bill finding a load of Class A in my motor on top of the shooting and the wounding.

I walked back up the gangplank a bit unsteadily and went aboard for ten minutes to get my head together and get our story straight for Mr Plod. Nobody had seen much anyway because they'd all been hiding but I told them that it was a plain case of self-defence because the bloke had been trying to murder me. I told the cops the gunman had got stabbed by someone 100 yards away and was now on his way to hospital. They searched the area and found the gun and the used cartridges. They confiscated my car for forensic testing and I was taken to the nick for questioning.

Then they came to us and said, 'Look, lads, we know you've got something to do with this stabbing because you've got specks of blood on your trousers.' They said they knew who Mr L was, a main crack-dealer, one of the top boys in London, and they knew there had been a row and he'd come back with a gun to kill us. It was pretty obviously self-defence.

I thought at this stage that Mr L had died. I'd last seen him lying motionless in a river of blood 10ft long. I didn't think anyone could survive a beating like that. He'd been stabbed up the arse, through his back and arms, half his stomach was hanging out. And he'd been beaten to a pulp with knuckledusters and baseball bats. This was underworld retribution at its most savage. I don't seek to justify it. It happens in the jungle that is London's underworld and that was the world I moved in. He'd come to kill us. We'd tried to kill him. Rough justice. That's the way it was.

Who, the cops wanted to know, could have inflicted such injuries, even on a scumbag crack-dealer who probably deserved it? Well, we didn't know, did we? We said we were hiding behind trees and bushes and ducking and diving to escape injury and had only got near the geezer to disarm him. We didn't see anyone knocking the shit out of him. It must have been another little firm who'd got the hump.

The senior officer had clearly guessed the truth. He said, 'Look, lads, it was obviously self-defence. We're on your side. Just make a statement and we can get it all tidied up.'

We said, 'Oh no, officer, all we know is that some black geezers came and started shooting up the place and we all hid.'

He didn't believe us but would never get the evidence for an attempted murder charge. As we were about to leave, another cop sidled up and said, 'If I were you, I'd get rid of all your clothes when you get home. We know this geezer, we know what he's been doing.' They seemed to be saying that if he did die, it would be no great loss to anyone and might save a few of the lives of the addicts he supplied.

Tony Tucker and me were best mates then and he drove all the way from Southend to pick me up from the nick. I'd phoned Denny, my girlfriend at the time, on my mobile, after the stabbing and told her to ring the solicitors and warn them I might be in trouble. I thought I was looking at a murder rap. Denny had phoned Tony and he was straight in his motor to collect me. That's how good a mate he was. He'd just dropped everything to help me.

The stabbing victim had five blood transfusions, dozens of

stitches, and spent two weeks in intensive care under a 24-hour armed guard. He was eventually charged with firearms offences and sent up to the Old Bailey for trial. They wanted me to be one of the prosecution witnesses. I wasn't happy with that. We had a meeting in a pub the Sunday before the trial and I told the other boys, 'I'm not going.'

They said, 'What, you'll be in deep shit.'

I didn't care, I told them, I wasn't going to court. I said, 'It's not the done thing. In our world, you live by the sword, you die by the sword.'

I didn't think any of us should go. I decided to bolt up at a secret address out of London while the police were trying to serve a witness summons on me at my home address. Then I heard what his defence was going to be in court. Me and him had had a fight at the club door and he'd beaten fuck out of me. I'd pulled out a knife and stabbed him and then pulled out a gun and shot up my own car and the boat. Like you would. It was fucking ludicrous. I thought the geezer was going to play it straight and keep his mouth shut. But, instead, he was going to slag me off.

On the third day of the trial, the cops went to my mum and dad's address and left a message saying that if I didn't turn up at the Old Bailey by 3.00 that afternoon they would issue a warrant for my arrest and charge me with the gun offences and the attempted murder of the dealer.

I thought then that I had to go. It wasn't worth the risk of being done with all that serious stuff just for not giving evidence.

So I was up there at the Bailey and they were asking me if I hadn't turned up because I had been threatened. I said, 'No, you just don't do that sort of thing. We have our own code we live by.'

I was now chief prosecution witness and set for some tough questioning. The defence barrister had apparently applied to drag my violent past out to discredit me but it hadn't been allowed. So to get round it his first question was 'Have you ever appeared on television, Mr Leach?'

He'd obviously seen the *Hooligans* documentary I'd been in and wanted me to say I'd taken part in it as a self-confessed thug. I replied, 'Yes, I've been on the telly, but the stand broke and I fell off.'

The judge was not amused and he bollocked me for being flippant. The barrister could see he was getting nowhere so he switched to the night of the gun attack. 'You say in your statement, Mr Leach, that all you could see coming towards you was a black man with a gold tooth.'

I said, 'But most black men have a gold tooth.'

He turned to the jury and gave them a big wide beaming smile and said, 'Members of the jury, you will note that I haven't.'

I said, 'Well, fuck me, you're the first black bloke I've seen without a gold tooth.'

Everyone started laughing and I got pulled up again by the judge. The barrister suggested that me and Mr L had been fighting and he'd been beating me. I said, 'Look, mate, no one would have got that close because if anyone gets within a couple of inches, I headbutt them.'

He claimed that I'd pulled the gun out of my car and started the shoot-up.

'Oh, fucking hell, yes you're right,' I said, 'then I pulled out another gun and John Wayne was there and we just rode past shooting at everyone.'

That brought me bollocking number three from the judge. The jury thought I was a right lunatic. The police were getting the right hump with me.

Then the defence barrister said to me, 'Is my client the man who shot you?'

I said, 'No, he's not.'

He looked startled. 'What? What are you saying?'

I said, 'How can I tell whether it's him? It was seven o'clock in the morning, still half dark, I was dog tired, all black men look the same to me. All I could see was a pair of white eyes and a gold tooth.'

The geezer in the dock looked at me in sheer disbelief. And suddenly his barrister was lost for words.

'No, that's definitely not him, it's a case of mistaken identity,' I added to rub salt into the wound.

Not surprisingly, I was dismissed from giving further evidence. As I walked out, Mr L gave me a half-nod. Then the Old Bill started giving me a right verbal monstering and the court refused to pay me any expenses for the day. Mr L had come back from the dead and now he'd walked out on a string of serious charges. My kind of justice.

I bumped into him two years later, after he'd been back to Manchester to some heavy-duty friends in the drug game, and had returned to London and started hitting the clubs.

Everyone was knocking him back out of respect for me. So I said, 'No, let him in.' I thought that all the time I knew where he was, I was safe from a revenge attack. If I didn't know, he could have hit me any time, anywhere, out of the blue.

Then, one night, I bumped into him at the Aquarium Club in Old Street. He limped over, a lasting result of his stabbing injuries, and I said, 'Right, how do you want to do it? Do you want to finish it here and now? If you do, I will kill you stone dead. You can end this feud now, call it a day, or one of us will die.'

To my surprise, he said, 'No, no, I want to buy you a drink. If it wasn't for you, I'd be doing ten years.'

He said his barrister had told him after the trial, 'Carlton Leach has saved your bacon. You owe him.'

So I accepted his truce; there was no point in prolonging that particular war and I knew now I wouldn't need to keep looking over my shoulder for a bullet coming my way.

So me and a bloke I'd nearly killed, who we'd beaten to within an inch of his life, stood shoulder to shoulder downing large vodkas like old mates. And I felt better about it. This was our code. We'd settled things our way, honour intact on both sides.

Then, suddenly, a fight kicked off in the club. People were yelling and knives were out. That was my kind of action and I waded in. To my surprise, Mr L joined me at my side. From the best of enemies, we were now fighting side by side, backs to the wall, looking after each other's interests. I got cut trying to stop two black geezers killing each other. I stepped in and got slashed across the arm. Now we were real blood brothers. He looked across at me and said, 'Fucking hell, mate, you don't half attract trouble.' That was true.

★   ★   ★

Whether I really attracted trouble, or it attracted me, I'm not sure – either way, there was no avoiding it. I was out with two of my boys, Gaffer and Fearless, and we'd been to Legends in the West End and then on to the EC1 club when we ran into a team known as The Rat Boys. I was suited and booted and had been having a social evening out chatting to a few doormen mates, so I wasn't looking for bother. I was ready to turn my back when trouble flared. But Gaffer jumped in and made himself double busy like he usually did. I shouted at him, 'Get back here, they've got good doormen of their own. Stay out of it. They're not having a go at us so keep your nose out of it.'

But the atmosphere had got nasty. Several people came over and asked if they could stand by us because they were frightened. Although I was in the muscle game, I'd always had an ability to keep calm and make people feel safe. About 20 or 30 people were standing next to me. Next thing, two shots rang out. One bloke had been hit. The Rat Boys had gone away and had tooled themselves up with guns and they'd come back looking to sort out the geezers they'd had the barney with. I thought, Oh no, not again. Mr L had been right, I did seem to attract trouble.

Another bloke had got shot, people were screaming, the police sirens were heading our way. This time, I stood there cool as a cucumber and said to Gaffer and Fearless, 'OK, boys, time to go home. We're in the wrong place at the wrong time. This is not our fight.'

With that, we calmly walked out through the door and left the fracas in our wake. This time, Captain Sensible was talking in my ear and we drove off and had a Chinese meal with no risk to any more of my nine lives. Gaffer said, 'How can you be so cool?'

I told him it was instinct, a front, in which I get this screen that comes over me and I could be in control in dangerous situations. Most of the time, anyway. People respect you for it. But I knew it was for my own survival as much as anything. I'd had too many friends die and the last couple of years had taught me lessons.

My good pal Black Francis had got shot outside the Frog and Nightgown in the Old Kent Road; Big Ron had been shot on his doorstep. Then Tony and the boys had been wiped out in the Rettendon murders. There had been too much grief, even in my dangerous world. I'd been with people in clubs and seen everyone getting edgy, it was like something really big was about to go off. Everyone seemed to be carrying a gun. It didn't frighten me, but I knew some day someone was going to come looking for my scalp. I was a bit of a name around the muscle scene and I was always going to be a target for some up-and-coming young bruiser who wanted to take me on because of who I was, not because of anything I'd done. Sooner or later, it was coming.

And I was becoming distrustful of my own friends; things were going on for money behind my back. I wasn't sure of the people around me any more. I was becoming lonely in a crowd. I was feeling weakened. And I thought now was the time to get out. But could I ever really escape?

I'd been around the club scene for more than ten years. I'd witnessed a lot of villainy, a lot of violence, monstrous, shocking acts of brutality. I'd always carried a big knife. I regarded it as one of the tools of the trade and I'd never been afraid to use it. Now guns were everywhere, not knives.

An old pal from West London, a bit of a face on his own manor, came up to me one night in a club just after I started going out with my current girlfriend Kelly and asked how I was. Then he dropped his voice and said, 'Got anything on you?'

I knew what he meant – any weapon? I said, 'No, no, I'm OK.'

Then he pulled a .38 out from under his shirt and said, 'Do you want this?'

No, I fucking didn't. And I didn't want this prick offering me guns in front of my girlfriend. I'd got my teenage daughter Carly there, too, and some family friends. He insisted, 'Take it, mate, a bit of protection.'

No thanks, pal, I'd seen too much damage done. But then I thought, Hold on, has this geezer heard something I don't know about? Does he think I need protection? He's not part of my normal circle but he seems to be picking up bad vibes involving me. What's going on? I told him, 'I'm all right, I don't need protection.'

But the doubt was there. I knew something sinister was in the air. What had it all come to now, geezers trying to flog me a shooter while I'm out with my family? Things weren't right. If you live in a world of criminals, there are only two places you are likely to end up – in prison or in the graveyard. And I didn't fancy either.

I knew that from the moment I put a gun in my pocket – and I'm not saying guns hadn't been in my possession a few times – I had to be prepared to use it. Guns aren't for show. They're the most powerful and destructive weapon you can have and too many hot-heads were touting them around. It would be easy to get into a silly argument with someone drugged up or drunk. He's carrying and he's pulled it out. Deep down, he doesn't want to shoot you but now he's the Terminator and he's got to use it to prove he's tough and hard. The proper people in the underworld do carry guns regularly. It's different when you are working. You are doing a job, it's controlled. Tony Tucker carried a shooter, but only for protection when he was busy on criminal activities. At the end of the day, it couldn't save him, could it?

There is an armoury of guns out there if you want them. They are hidden away, buried or stashed, sitting there 'til someone needs one, then destroyed or put back safely, depending on whether they've been used or not and might be carrying incriminating evidence. If they've been fired, they are best out of the way. I can get shooters from my connections at any time of the night or day and I wouldn't hesitate to do so if anyone hurt my children or any of my family. Come and hurt me any time, but stay away from my family. That's personal and that has a different code. The street has got its own laws, its own politics, and that's the way it rumbles. But drugs are changing a lot of that. With drugs go lunatics, loaded guns and no principles, no underworld codes, no honour among thieves.

There is no doubt that drugs changed my life, too. I started taking steroids to build up my body, to get those rippling biceps, that bull neck, to be the toughest guy in clubland bursting out of my dinner jacket and bow-tie. And I ended up becoming a monster. I was the Incredible Hulk who could turn from nice guy to raging maniac in seconds. Just one wrong word or if my toast wasn't done right. Any small thing and I was off on one. From taking the mild steroid Anovar, I got hooked on stronger and stronger doses. I'd look in the mirror in the morning and see my muscles getting bigger and bigger, rippling with power like someone out of a Mr Universe contest.

I had a really bad car crash in the late Eighties which laid me up for months. I needed to build myself up afterwards and I started taking the heavy-duty steroids, injecting testosterone and Sustenon, anything I could get my hands on, oblivious to any damage, mental or physical, they might do. I'd always looked after myself, trained regularly, played a lot of football, so it wasn't as if I was a seven-stone weakling trying to build myself up to beat the beach bullies. No, I wanted more than fit. I wanted big. I wanted people to say, 'Wow! Look at that geezer. He looks the business.' And, of course, the bigger you were, the tougher you looked, the more the work kept rolling in. And, yes, I've got to admit that vanity played a big part. Doormen are the vainest people in the world. You are on parade and you need to look the part. I was Schwarzenegger.

I was Stallone. And it's definitely a turn-on for the women, too. I've lost count of the times I got approached for sex while I was on the door.

The downside of steroids is the terrible neurosis, the paranoia, the short fuse, the terrifying rages. I would get involved in near-psychopathic road-rage incidents all the time. If someone cut me up or did the wanker gesture, I'd go after them like a madman. I once ripped the door off a car to get to a bloke who cut me up on a roundabout. I chased him for five miles before I caught him. He was fucking petrified. Another geezer shouted something out of the window of his motor in Dagenham so I pulled across him at the next lights. He locked his doors from inside so I put my fist straight through the windscreen.

Another time, someone had parked in my space outside the Paradise Club. So I got a few of my blokes out, all beefy sorts, and we took a corner of the car each and just bounced it down the road. As we were shunting it along, the owners came back. They stood open-mouthed as they watched us heaving it about like it was a lump of plastic or something. I said, 'Sorry, mate, but you were illegally parked.' He wasn't about to start an argument with six heavyweight bouncers over his parking rights.

I now know steroids are the most dangerous drugs I have ever taken in my life, and the damaging effects of my abuse will be with me 'til the day I die.

★   ★   ★

I used to take steroid courses six weeks on, six weeks off. But I found that over the six weeks I wasn't injecting them, I would start to feel weakened, my body was craving for more and more. Sometimes I'd take more even though I knew it could be dangerous medically.

Because my body had become so big and strong I constantly needed more food. I remember the first time it happened was while we were shopping at Lakeside. My whole body started shaking, demanding food to satisfy the steroid-induced hunger. It was like shovelling coal on to a blazing fire. After that, I always carried screwtop jars of Heinz baby food around with me for a quick food fix. They contained all the nutrients and vitamins my body was crying out for. I'd take loads with me, all flavours – beef, ham, chicken – and guzzle them down six at a time, even when I was working. I know I wasn't the only baby food junkie either. I'd got the tip from a pal on steroids and he told me dozens of bodybuilders were whacking down baby food. It made sense to me and it helped because it was so quickly digested by the system.

But it didn't do a lot for my foul tempers. One day, Denny served me up a meal that was about the size of a child's dinner. I went berserk. I yelled at her, 'How the fuck am I supposed to live on that?' I hurled the plate across the room and it smashed against a wall. I dragged the fridge out and turned it over. I smashed up the kitchen causing hundreds of pounds' worth of damage. And all for nothing. Just pointless rage. I picked up a baseball bat and was smashing myself across the head with it. My rage had reached such ferocity that I feared I would kill Denny if I didn't vent my anger on myself.

Another time, I picked up a settee and threw it across the room like it was a kid's toy. I'd lost control of that terrible violence inside me and my family were suffering. I put them through hell. I'd put a gun to Denny's head, I'd held a knife to her throat. That's how bad it was. I was a walking time-bomb and dangerous to be near. No wonder she eventually kicked me out.

At that period in my life, with steroids as my master and vanity as my partner, I was probably the most selfish, horrible person you could ever meet. I was out there with my mates, 20-stone monsters with 20in biceps, and getting a buzz when people looked at us in absolute awe as we walked 15-handed into a club or pub.

Back home, I was on an emotional helter-skelter, up and down, up and down, terrible mood swings, sleepless nights, four-day nose bleeds, taking coke for the all-night doors and feeling my blood pressure surging out of control 'til my head was almost bursting.

In short, steroids have left my body fucked. With fantastic help from Kelly, who's only half my age but twice as strong, I'm clean of all illicit drugs now. But I still take pills for blood pressure, my liver is constantly monitored by the doctor, most of my organs have been pushed beyond their limits and I've probably shortened my life by 10 or 15 years. I could go back into training, I could go back on steroids and get back to 17 or 18 stone and look brilliant, but inside, the doctors say, I would have the organs of a 60-year-old man. The heart can only take so much. It's a muscle and when you take steroids it grows and grows to keep pace with your physique. You can end up having a heart-attack, and when they do the post mortem they find out you've got the heart of an old man and you've worn it out. I owe it to Kelly and my kids to stay clean, stay in control, stay alive.

The moment is still vivid in my memory of the day that I had passed the point of no return and given up hope of ever getting my life straight. I'd had a big bust-up with Kelly after I'd dragged her out of a party and terrified the 200 guests so much that even the doormen had locked themselves in their car. Kelly is a really pretty redhead with a lovely slim figure and a great smile. I knew other men looked at her and fancied her. They probably wondered what the hell she was doing with a lump like me, twice her age. I should have been proud that she was so attractive to the opposite sex. But that green-eyed monster got the better of me and all I felt was raging jealousy if another bloke looked at her.

After the party bust-up, Kelly didn't want to see me again. No one wanted to know me. I knew I'd gone too far this time. I'd become a wild animal people were too scared to go near.

I got myself a gun, went to my mum and dad's home and sat in the box room absolutely desolate. I sat for an hour looking at the shooter on my lap, then picked it up and put it in my mouth. I thought, Fuck it, I'm fed up with this world. I'm 40 years of age and what have I got? Nothing.

I'd had four serious, long-term relationships, nice houses, four kids by different women, but what did it all mean now? I felt a lonely, broken man. I reckoned everybody looked on me as a low-life drunk, a no-hoper, and I might as well go and join my mates down the cemetery. I could see no solution other than to pull the trigger.

I cocked the gun, then a voice told me, 'No, that's the coward's way out, Carlton.' Suddenly, I was imagining the horror my parents would suffer if they came home and found me dead with my brains splashed all over the ceiling. The voice in my head was telling me, 'Why not prove everybody wrong? Show them what you are made of.' I knew Tony's dad, Ronald, had died there and then from shock at his home in Folkestone, Kent, when he was told about the Rettendon murders. He was only 63, no age these days for anyone to die. I couldn't bear the thought of that happening to my dear Dad, he didn't deserve that. Neither did Mum. And what about my lovely kids? They couldn't have handled their dad topping himself. Not big, tough Dad, who always came up with the money at birthday time.

I looked at their photos and said, 'No, this is not the way.' I'd always been a fighter and I'd fight my way back from this. For my family if for nobody else. I knew I had to start again, drag myself up from the pits of despondency and make myself a better man. Nobody could help me but myself. It was time to boot out all the self-pity.

I picked myself up, threw the gun away and headed for the doctor's surgery. His grim prognosis was everything I had dreaded: 'Carry on with your present lifestyle, Mr Leach, and you are going to die. No beating about the bush. You *will* die.'

Now I really needed help. I was put on a specialist course

to dry me out, build me up, cleanse my body of the steroids, cleanse my mind of the depressions and paranoia. It was many long months before I could see the light at the end of the tunnel and an end to the darkest days of my life.

★   ★   ★

Having cheated death at the business end of Mr L's Browning, and my own shooter in my parents' box room, I know now that I should have been the fourth victim in the headline-making Rettendon murders, alongside my best mate Tony Tucker, and two other members of our firm, Pat Tate and Craig Rolfe, when they were gunned down in that Range Rover. And I'm still haunted today by the knowledge that my name is on a bullet and someone could be waiting for me any time, any day, to finish the job. That's why I live in a home with secure access only, and when I walk out of the door I check there's no one suspicious hanging around. No bastard's coming to take me by surprise. They might be waiting out there for me one dark night, but I won't go down without a fight, that's for sure. I suppose it's the price I've got to pay for getting caught up in one of the most notorious multiple murders in England.

I was one of the first people hauled in for questioning after the shootings. Because I hadn't been with the victims, the Old Bill thought I must have had something to do with it. I told them that was crap. Tony was a great mate — why would I want to see him topped? I'll tell you later what I think really happened that dreadful night when the boys had their brains blown out.

Up 'til then, we'd been ruling Essex like we owned the fucking place. If anyone tried to cross our paths or move in on our business deals, we'd destroy them. It was a brutal, evil world, and I was fuelled up most of the time on a cocktail of booze, drugs and adrenalin. We thought we were invincible. I was so hyped up there were times when I thought, literally, that bullets would bounce off my body. The others were the same.

We muscled up on steroids to try to look like like Arnold fucking Schwarzenegger, doing coke and speed to see us through night after night without sleep. Most of the time, the four of us went everywhere together and I would almost certainly have been in that Range Rover with them on the night they were shot if they had felt they were in danger – but they hadn't asked, so they must have felt safe.

How wrong could they have been? I'm sure I was as much an intended target as the other three. They wanted the whole firm out of the way. I can't believe I'm here today to write this book. I just hope I'm still around to finish it.

We had become wild bastards in the Eighties and early Nineties. We had a huge network of bodybuilders who worked for us as club doormen and minders and enforcers, any kind of rough stuff. By controlling club doors, we could control who was running the drugs inside and we made dealers cough up £1,000 a time to operate in the top places. We were raking in a fortune and spending it like there was no tomorrow. Life was one long party. We always went out tooled up — knuckle dusters, coshes, knives. It was as routine as brushing your teeth. For a really serious job, we'd think nothing of packing a 9mm pistol. We had respect – or, I suppose, I'd call it fear now – at every place we went into in Essex. Nobody messed with us. Life was a permanent buzz.

I had become addicted to violence, the threat of violence, the idea of violence. There were big drug deals going on, some I knew about, others I didn't, and all the time there was a simmering undercurrent of distrust and hatred building up ready to erupt in open warfare. Too many people were taking too many drugs and all sensible reason was out of the window.

Once, we went to buy some nicked travellers' cheques, worth about £250,000, from another firm of villains up in East London. They kept messing us about, changing the dates and times of the meet. So Tony decided we'd kidnap the fuckers to teach them a lesson. We arranged a meet in an out-of-the-way car park in Woodford. Some of us were carrying 9mm guns and the usual assortment of tools. Me and Pat waited until Tony gave the signal then all hell broke loose. I grabbed the ringleader and pummelled him in the head while Tony and Pat smashed up the others. Pat started hitting one bloke so hard he sent him flying through the air and on to the roof of a car, setting the alarm off. Lights started going on all round us so we ran to our cars and scarpered leaving the other lot lying about, battered and bloody. It was all in a typical night's work for the Essex Boys. Total disregard for law and order. I'll tell you more about the terrifying consequences of this job on another Essex villain later on.

We lived like kings and partied like animals. We spent fortunes on tailor-made clothes and ran about in Porsches,

Mercs and BMWs. Women seemed attracted by the aura of violence and they threw themselves at us wherever we went, and I mean really good-looking girls, not Essex-girl slappers.

Pat Tate's appetite for sex was legendary. He'd just been released from prison once when a gunman blasted him at his home and badly injured him. He was rushed into hospital bleeding badly and put into a ward all rigged up with tubes, bandages and plasters. Still it didn't stop him wanting his end away, even when he was in traction. From his bed, he phoned up for hookers to visit him and got up to all sorts. He thought it was hilarious.

We were all pushing our luck with drugs. The night I came face to face with Mr L's Browning, I was so pumped up on steroids and cocaine I felt I could walk through walls.

The terrible thing about drugs is that you don't realise when you are on them how stupid they make you. I deserved to be shot that night. I behaved like a fucking lunatic. But that's the way things were, just one small example of the way we were running out of control. We were getting up the noses of a lot of people but we couldn't see the dangers brewing up all around us.

When I heard that Tony, Pat and Craig had all been wiped out on an Essex farm track just before Christmas 1995, it shook me rigid. I knew I had to take stock of my life, and get my head clear of all the shit that was going on in there.

It was three years before the killers were finally brought to justice and that gave me time for a long, cold, clinical look at where I was. My best mate was dead; my head was done in with drugs; my liver and kidneys had been fucked by steroids, and I would need medical treatment for the rest of my life, however long that might be; my marriage was on the rocks; and every relationship I'd ever had was wrecked by philandering and paranoia. Not a great track record.

I know that the men who were convicted of killing the boys, Micky Steele and Jack Whomes, are banged up for life but I can't shake the fear that I might be the next one to catch a bullet if old scores are going to be settled. The murders were supposed to have happened after Tony, Pat and Craig had been lured to that farm track on a bogus drugs deal. Maybe yes, maybe no – whatever happened, they paid too great a price. Meanwhile, I'm keeping my head down and trying to rebuild the shattered remnants of my life, making sure I'm one jump ahead of any bastard that comes looking for me.

It's been 20 years of violence, from a tearaway on the football terraces to fully-fledged thug, and I just wish now I could turn back the clock. Maybe if I'd stayed at the job I was trained for, marine engineering, it might have been different. But I got caught up in the culture of violence, and violence itself is a lethal drug. I chose that world; I've got to live with the consequences.

It started when a club in Stratford had a doorman knocked out one Friday night and had no one to mind the door on the Saturday and they asked if I fancied it. I'd already got a reputation as a hard-case West Ham supporter and they knew I could handle myself. Fancy it? Like a duck to water.

Terrific. I was 21 years old, fit as a fiddle and here I was doing door work in a bow-tie. I was Jacko. It was like a fantastic, exciting game to me. Then the drug culture arrived in clubland and the world all changed. And I had become trapped in the middle of a vicious spiral of drugs and violence that was to take me to the heights of perceived invincibility and to the depths of total despair.

I was lured into this world, strangely, by the supposed safe drug Ecstasy. I was doing door work when the rave party boom came along in the Eighties. I remember looking down on 8,000 people dancing in a warehouse in East London that had been taken over by some underground rave organisers. There were some hard people there – boxers, violent people, soccer hooligans I knew – but everyone was loving each other. Nobody was giving bother. I'd been in clubs with 200 people and been in fights three times a night. But now we'd got a new phenomenon. All these people full of love and peace. It made the hairs on the back of my neck stand up. I'd never experienced a feeling like it. I was in my late twenties by then and, honestly, hand on heart, had never taken a drug of any sort. Looking at that mass of people all holding each other in a sort of universal embrace at four o'clock in the morning, smiling, happy, kissing and hugging, not wanting to go home, I knew I had to try one. It intrigued me, I wanted to know.

That was the night I was seduced by lady Ecstasy and my life was to change for ever. My eyes fixed on the strobe lights and I was tripping. I was in another world. All I wanted to do was talk to people, be nice. The tough soccer lout, the brawny doorman, became a hippy tripper. I was thinking to myself, This is great.

I couldn't really explain it. I'd worked in clubs in London, North, East, South and West and everyone was at each other's throats, but this was lovely. I couldn't believe 8,000 people could be together all night and there was no aggro. No wonder the Americans had given the same tablets to their Vietnam veterans to help conquer the terrible traumas of war. They were then class A, medically-prescribed drugs to help the soldiers cope with flashbacks and nightmares and, to date, had few side-effects. Now they had arrived in Britain as a party drug and the crooks were cashing in. It was only a matter of time before bad gear was being produced and someone was going to die. The inevitable happened, and usually it was a pretty girl who took the fatal dose. Then came the death of the ex-policeman's daughter Leah Betts in Essex and the Ecstasy culture was in the headlines and our firm was being linked to the tragedy amidst a surge of public outrage.

If I hadn't taken that tablet, if I'd just said no, I don't think I'd have taken the path I did, would never have got mixed up in the drug world, and never done the terrible things I did. It was probably the most stupid thing I ever did. But because I started taking it, somehow I convinced myself it was right. From a £40-a-night club doorman, I was suddenly in the drug scene big time with money sloshing about everywhere, looking after rave promotors, loads of drink, unlimited Es and slowly but surely the door was being opened to bigger and seedier things. Then came the big stepping stone to the heavier stuff and the gang wars and the violence and then murder and it could all have been avoided if I'd turned my back on one small pill. Whatever the experts say, there's no doubt in my mind that one drug leads to another, up and up the ladder 'til all you can do is fall off. I've been there, seen it, I've had that ultimate buzz and then gone looking for something better, something new. Now it sickens me.

I'll never forget the day just before the murders when I went to my mate Tony's house and saw him out of his head and injecting cocaine into a vein. Here was a man who was so proud of his body, a fitness fanatic, and there he was pulling down his shirt sleeves trying to hide 30 fucking needle holes from me. I was shocked. But then I'd got no room to criticise. I was on steroids for years and, in my opinion, they are the worst drugs of all, by far. The emotional and physical side-effects are catastrophic. You can become impotent or you can go the other way and become sex addict. That's the way I went. I became a rampant superstud. I wanted to fuck eight, nine or ten times a day. I had two girls on the go at the same time then but still wasn't satisfied.

That caused problems with relationships when I started looking elsewhere. I was a horrible, revolting sexual predator, but couldn't see it.

I've seen six or seven mates die in the last six years. I've seen a lot of things and I've done a lot of things. I've been to a lot of funerals. Now I've won my toughest battle and got clean of drugs and for the sake of my kids and my girlfriend and the few people who still believe in me I've got to make sure my funeral is not the next one.

2

Carnage

Anna's screams will haunt me 'til the day I die. Long agonised howls of despair as she learned the terrible truth about the savage murder of her lover, and my best pal, Tony Tucker. In those few minutes, on a bitterly cold December day in 1995, I became embroiled in one of the most notorious gangland killings in criminal history. Initially, I became the number-one suspect. I was under constant police surveillance for weeks. And I went on my own quest for revenge, intent on wiping out the bastards who'd taken Tony's life.

The first I knew that something was wrong was a phone call at about 10.30 in the morning from a mate saying, 'I think something's happened to Tony and the boys.'

I said, 'What do you mean? What sort of thing?'

'Something bad,' he said.

He'd heard something on the grapevine but wasn't saying much in case it was wrong. I switched on the radio to catch the news. It was there on the 11.00am bulletin. 'The bodies of three men have been found in a Range Rover on a farm at Rettendon in Essex ...'

I shuddered. I knew Tony, Pat and Craig used a Range Rover. I even remembered the number – F424 NPE. I knew they'd been planning a bit of secret business in Essex. But surely, they couldn't be dead. The Essex Boys were invincible, weren't they?

I rang Andy who worked for Tony in one of his health shops. 'Have you heard anything?' I asked.

'No, mate,' he said.

I was getting really really bad vibes by now. 'Can you go round and see Tony's missus to see if she knows anything?' I asked.

'Sure, mate,' he said.

He phoned half-an-hour later. He was with Anna. She hadn't seen Tony since the previous night but that wasn't unusual and she had no reason to worry.

'Oh, Christ, mate, the police have just arrived,' he told me on the mobile. 'They're at the door. They are talking to Anna now.'

Then I heard the awful screams in the background as Anna's world collapsed around her. I slumped on to my bed sobbing like a baby, confused, distraught, fearful. This, I knew, was just the start of a dreadful nightmare. And the police quickly made it clear that they thought this could be the onset of a vicious gangland war with more bloodshed to be expected.

I'd been a close pal of Tony Tucker's for five years so it was no surprise that Old Bill were on my doorstep within a matter of hours. We were both from the back streets of East London and vaguely knew each other as kids. We met up again at his shop in Ilford where he sold bodybuilding gear, sports equipment and health foods and had a security outfit in the back offices supplying doormen for nightclubs. He was doing really well. He was shrewd in business and highly successful with his turnover from providing club doormen, earning in excess of £5,000 a week.

There was instant mutual respect when we met up in the early Nineties. We were both fit, both bodybuilders and shared the same interests in life – birds, booze and parties. He was shrewd with people, too. He didn't tolerate fools gladly and was quick to make judgements about people he had only just met. I thought he was often too harsh with people, but he wasn't often wrong.

'Be careful, Carl,' he said, 'most people are only using you. Don't trust anyone.'

It was ironic that on the night he was killed, he'd gone down a lonely country lane in the dead of night. He had clearly trusted someone and they had blown him to kingdom come. That's what brought the cops to my doorstep. It didn't take them long to find out that we were best mates and Tony had obviously been double-crossed by someone he'd believed to have been a good pal.

'We need to talk to you to eliminate you from our enquiries,' which really means, 'We think you might have done it.'

'Where were you last night?'

I was in deep shock. I was worried. I was angry and I didn't want to tell them anything. Quite frankly, my first thoughts were that the Old Bill themselves had killed the boys. The tragic death of policeman's daughter Leah Betts from Ecstasy a few months earlier triggered rumours that this was a brutal revenge, shot down a dark lane to try to make it look like some sort of drugs war. I was horrified that they were now considering me as a suspect.

'Why the fuck would I murder my best mate?' I asked them.

I didn't tell them how close me and Tony were. At that moment in time, I wasn't saying anything to anybody because I didn't trust anybody. If they'd dug around they'd have found out the obvious, that me and Tony did a bit of security work together, that we partied a lot together and were the best of mates. There had been a lot of mutual favours; Tony would give me moody invoices for security jobs to keep the tax man happy and I'd helped him out with a club he was minding in Wandsworth and needed to sort some bother with a little team of local villains. I took some of my boys up there and dealt with it. We stood beside Tony like Mafia hoodlums. The locals thought I'd taken over the door, but I told them, 'No, I'm just a friend, but if you take on Tony, take on us as well.'

We were both doing well out of the muscle business. I'd got my own company – Renaquest – doing club doors, concerts, sports events, that sort of thing, and made enough to live well. Tony rented me an office next to his premises in

Ilford and we sort of worked side by side for a few years. I was doing OK but what I made I spent. If I made £10,000, £20,000 or £30,000 I'd spunk it all away. But Tony had the style and the business brain. He knew how to turn over real money and make it work for him; he knew how to run a company for a year, then liquidate it, and swap the directors about so no one knew where the cash was going, least of all the tax man. He was really on the ball, fit, sharp, going places. A real professional. He was the one with the big house, the smart accountant, the flash cars and serious money in the bank.

We used to joke that he was like a Mafia Godfather character and I'd call him Tony Mancino for a laugh and he loved it.

I was in his office one day when Nigel Benn phoned and asked him to do the security for his next fight. I'd already met Nigel's brother Danny when we were training in the same gym in Forest Gate when we were teenagers. Later on, when Nigel had just come out of the Army and was getting ready for his first pro fight, Danny introduced me to him at the Room at the Top in Ilford, so we had met briefly. We'd chatted a few times since, while I was doing the door at clubs like Astair's and Echoes, so we were on chatting terms and now Nigel was really making the big time as a fighter with world title ambitions. He'd said a couple of times that if I needed a bit of work to give him a ring. But I'd never been someone to jump on the bandwagon and hadn't taken him up on it.

Tony didn't know I knew Nigel and Nigel didn't know

I knew Tony, and Nigel didn't know anything about our criminal activities. He'd bought his vitamins, iron tablets, and other similar legal supplements off him when he was in training.

Tony was more than happy to do the security for the next fight. It was the needle match return fight against Chris Eubank in 1993, the one the entire British public were waiting for. Tony said, 'Oh, I've got my mate Carlton here with me,' and Nigel said, 'I know Carlton. Bring him along for the fight.'

That was the start of a three-way friendship that lasted through Nigel's career up 'til Tony's murder. Tony respected Nigel as a boxer but also liked him as a person. Once, Nigel was having some minor trouble with his wife Sharron, and Tony was having woman trouble as well and Nigel went to Tony's house and they sat and had a good moan and a few tears. They really gelled together. Then there was me, totally different again, but we all really bonded and became great mates. They were good times.

We'd do the fight security together, I'd go with Nigel when he took the pre-fight blood tests or when he went to the toilet or changing rooms and we'd walk him into the ring. There was a young handicapped boy called Tim whom Nigel had befriended and whatever happened in a fight the first thing Nigel would do was see him and give him a kiss and he liked us to help Tim get backstage. He's a great human being, Nigel. He loved that kid and the boy loved him.

On the night of the Gerald McClellan fight at the London

Arena in 1995, Tim was there as usual, and Nigel's second wife, Carolyne, but there was trouble brewing early. I needed to make sure everyone was going to be safe. We walked Nigel to his corner. When the fight started, I went to keep Carolyne and Tim company because you can't see much from behind the corner. There was this big black security guard barring my way. Then Nigel hit the deck in round one and looked in trouble. Carolyne jumped up worried and leant forward. Natural enough. This black geezer started pushing her back. I said, 'Hey, don't do that, it's his missus.' She sat down and held my hand. It was a vicious war going on in the ring. With every punch I could feel her squeezing me, taking the pain for Nigel. The black security guy stood right in front of Tim. Then Nigel turned the fight round and knocked McClellan out with some brilliant punches. We were all cheering and yelling and got up at the ringside cuddling Nigel. There were 13,000 people in there all going mad.

Right in the middle of it, the black bloke tells me I've got to get off the ringside. I said, 'Don't you put your hands on me ...' Tempers were flaring and Nigel could see what was happening. Even with all the pandemonium going on he came across and told the bloke, 'Hey, lay off, he's security.' The bloke wouldn't take no for answer and he was trying to push me off the ring. He said something, I can't really remember what it was, so – Bang! I headbutted him and splattered his nose. Tony was also on the outside edge of the stage holding on to the ropes and I shouted, 'Oh fuck, I've nutted him.'

The bloke tried to have another go and push me off.

There were TV cameramen trying to film it for millions of Sky viewers to see, so we ducked out of their way because we didn't want the bad publicity. Then the teamwork snapped into action. As the bloke reeled back, trying to keep a foothold, Tony hit him – Crack! – and he took off, right up in the air and where has he landed? Right on the judges' table. This huge fucking lump had splattered right down in front of them. And they were all in their bow-ties looking up to see what's happening.

We were busy now trying to do a damage limitation job. I was holding a bloody great gash on my forehead. Frank Bruno had seen what was happening and he came over to see if he could help. It was fucking mayhem. I was bleeding, the black guy was bleeding from a busted nose and lying on the judges' table, McClellan was still unconscious in the ring, so we needed to get Nigel out to safety.

Then through the commotion, Nigel's cuts man, Dennie Mancini, clocked what had happened and came across to give me first aid treatment and stop the bleeding. I mean, the claret was just gushing down my face. It was like I'd headbutted a brick wall. The atmosphere was evil and getting worse. Then as Nigel was doing a TV interview, the black geezer was there again, staggering up in front of me, his face all busted up, and he's standing there, arms folded, threatening me, challenging me. By now I was really pissed off. So I said, 'Tell you what, I'll let you do me from behind,' and turned my back. The tension was unbelievable. I could hear someone in the crowd shouting, 'Carl, Carl ...' There were a lot of geezers there who would have known me so I wasn't too surprised. Then someone, or something, was tapping the back of my hands. I looked down and someone was pushing a knife my way. It had been passed down through the crowd, past the security boys, by somebody who obviously thought I was in serious trouble. I looked at the blade, pushed it away and said, 'No, I don't need that.' It vanished back into the crowd. I thought, Thank fuck for that, I don't want to be seen on prime-time TV cutting a bloke up. That's a sure recipe for a five stretch.

Things were calming down a bit and McClellan was taken off to hospital and Nigel was walking from the ring. He was a proud man and wanted to do it on his own, head held high. Every bit of him was hurting. He whispered to me, 'Carl, don't let go of me.' He was like jelly, his legs were buckling under him. We walked him out through the crowd and he'd gone. I thought he was dying.

Me and Tony carried him into the ambulance and he flinched in agony every time we touched him. My job was done and Nigel was on his way to the doctor's. By now, everyone was looking for me and Tony over the fight we'd had with the black guy. We rushed upstairs to Nigel's changing room and Dennie Mancini did a full cuts job on my injuries, cleaned me up, put some plasters on and slipped us out through a side door.

'There's fucking uproar going on over you two,' he said, 'get out before they find you.'

We didn't need a second invitation. We were in our motor and away.

★   ★   ★

All those memories of Tony and our wild times came flooding back as I tried to come to terms with the fact that he was dead. My best mate, my soul mate, blasted to death in cold blood. Never given a chance. Shot down like a rabid dog. I couldn't believe it. I cried for a week. I drank for a week. And I got angry for a week. Then I was ready to go looking for some answers.

I'd no idea Tony and the boys had been in such danger. Yes, we lived a risky life, took chances, pulled a few scams, but it was all a game to me. It was like being on the outside of a gangster movie looking in. Now I was hearing hardened coppers telling me I fitted the profile of the sort of bloke that could do this terrible thing. I was, they said, regarded as a hardened gangster with big-time crime connections. Was this really me?

What sort of world had I got myself into?

It was obvious that the police hadn't got a clue who was behind the triple murder. Neither had I. Nor had any of the mates I spoke to. I was getting sick of people asking me. I felt they were pointing the finger – 'You were his best mate, you must know.' I wracked my brains day after day trying to remember people we'd met, places we'd been, deals we'd done, in the hope of a clue. I knew that if I found the killers first, I would have no qualms about exacting my own retribution. But nothing came to me.

Somewhere in a distant memory, I recalled meeting a bloke known as Micky the Pilot. 'Blinding geezer,' I remember Tony saying, 'but he's paranoid as fuck and his house has got more security cameras than Fort Knox.' It didn't seem important. Not then, not yet.

After the Rettendon murders, I was doing a lot of thinking, wondering which people, which events, might be significant and I remembered how Tony had changed so much in the months before his death, how he had become a contradiction of everything he stood for. Health, fitness, reliability were out the window, and he was on the slippery slope of serious drug abuse. One event that kept coming to mind was a night at the Ministry of Sound, which was then my top door job, when a bloke called Bernie Mahoney got stabbed.

Through one of my regular doormen, Dave Dunne, he said he wanted to meet me. It was a meeting more dramatic than most – he turned up bleeding from a knife wound in his stomach. He was lying on the toilet floor writhing in agony.

I suspected right away who might have done it, a mixed-race geezer who I'd banned once but he'd come back screaming up my name as a mate and he'd been given a second chance. He was a right nasty fucker and I soon found him, with the bloodstained knife still on him. So I was sure he'd done it. He denied it.

I shouted at him, 'Don't fucking lie to me. You've been barred once, we've let you back, now you're taking the piss. I'm responsible for security here and you've shown me total disrespect.'

With that, he tried to stab one of my doormen and he

pulled out a CS gas canister. So I grabbed hold of him, hit him, and threw him into a small anteroom, not much bigger than a cage, near the club entrance. I grabbed an iron bar covered in a bit of rubber, and battered his head so badly he needed 56 stitches. I was like a raving lunatic. It was at a time when I was doing steroids big time, doing all sorts of drugs, and I'd completely lost it. It took ten blokes to drag me off him, otherwise I would have battered him to death. I was out of control, like a wild animal.

In that world, respect is all important and he had shown total disrespect. After the battering with the cosh, I grabbed a chair and started belting him over the head with that. The other doormen had to grab him by the ankles and drag him out through the club to get him away from me. They took him out of the back exit, put him in a car and a pal called Mark drove him off into the night and dumped him near where lived. I heard him saying to the geezer, 'Where do you live? Where do you live?' The injured bloke could hardly talk but managed to whisper Kilburn through blood-spattered teeth and Mark shoved him in the boot and took him off. It was a big favour because the police were outside the front of the club and if they'd known what had gone on I'd have been on a ten-year stretch for attempted murder. I saw that Bernie was OK and I calmed down and got back to business as normal.

The Ministry of Sound was the top London nightspot then and we got a fair bit of aggravation now and again, but I'd never lost it like that before and I hope I never will again. It scared me shitless, realising what I was capable of.

I saw Bernie several times after that terrifying introduction. He kept turning up at places we were doing the door. He always had a camera, always wanted his photo taken with the faces on the club scene. I didn't trust the guy. Take my photo on holiday in Spain, yes, but don't stick a camera in my face when I'm working a door. He turned up again when Nigel went to open the Academy Gym in Southend. It was owned by a good friend of mine and Nigel agreed to do the grand opening as a favour. There was Bernie again, camera at the ready.

Then I remember well the night in July 1994 when Pat Tate came out of prison. We'd organised a big homecoming party on the Sunday evening at the Epping Country Club. A big team turned out ... there must have been 50 of us out in the jungle. There were tasty types from all over Essex. I mean, any sensible normal person wouldn't have come near us. There was serious muscle out to play. We were all having a good time, getting drunk, having a party. And there was Bernie again, wanting pictures taken with Pat and Tony and me. I wouldn't let him. It didn't ring right to me. What was his game?

Next time I saw him was at Raquel's nightclub in Basildon which was to become notorious over the Leah Betts Ecstasy tragedy. The pills that killed her came from the club and it became the focal point of the police hunt for the pushers behind the racket. Bernie had been doing the door there, his own little bit of the security market, and we chatted a bit and he said he needed some invoices to keep the tax man happy. He tried to tap Tony up for some dodgy bills and receipts.

Tony came to me afterwards and said, 'I don't trust him, Carl.'

Then Bernie got us some visiting orders to go and see Reggie Kray in prison. He was a regular visitor to Reg, and various other notorious criminals, and had got hold of two VOs, brandishing them like royal decrees. But I didn't want to be like everyone else saying, 'Oh yes, I've been to see Reggie Kray.'

I had the greatest respect for him, and Ronnie, they were icons to me, the originals. I was brought up with the Kray folklore in the East End, but I didn't want to be on this bandwagon. I said to Tony, 'We'll give him respect, but we'll do it from a distance,' and we never went, even though Bernie was pushing it.

All these incidents were swirling round in my head as I tried to fit the jigsaw together. I didn't know what was important, what wasn't. But I knew that somewhere there must be clues to this assassination of my pals. And I knew that I was in too deep for my own good. My name was hot in the gangland scene. I was into a lot of stuff inside the clubs and out. People were getting stabbed, people were getting killed on the doors. My name was being brought up too much for comfort.

Tony's death was a wake-up call. I should have known where everything was leading but I was blind to the stupidity of it all. Now I'd got three mates in a mortuary. I had suspected in the few weeks before the murders that Tony and Pat were up to something. They'd become very secretive.

Two weeks before the shootings, it was Tony's fortieth birthday and we'd all gone up to Hollywood's nightclub in

Romford for a piss-up. I had had a gut feeling that night, a bad feeling, that something wasn't right. Pat seemed to be splitting up the friendship, the special bond between me and Tony. Right from the moment he came out, there was a spontaneous combustion between the two of them, a dangerous reaction you felt could explode at any minute. The trust between me and Tony was evaporating.

We'd made a pact one night that I would look after him and he would look after me and if either of us went off for a bit of business on our own, we'd let the other know. If I got into a dodgy situation, I knew Tony would cover my arse and vice versa. If I disappeared, or he disappeared, we'd know where to start looking. But that was all changing. I asked him what was going on.

He said, 'I'm on to something very, very big, but don't worry, mate, I'll look after you.'

I knew that was true. The previous Christmas I'd done a bit of business for Tony and taken him £2,800 in notes to his home. I'd hit a bit of a rough spot, because I was always silly with my spending, treated everyone, and he knew it. Tony put the £2,800 on the table and he said, 'You're skint, aren't you?'

I said, 'No, mate, I'm OK.'

But he knew. He said, 'Here, take the twenty-eight hundred quid. You and the kids have a good Christmas on me.'

Now what sort of friend does that? I loved him for it. He knew I was struggling and I couldn't hide it from him. There wasn't anything we could hide from each other. Or so I thought.

It was only after the murders that the dangerous secrets he harboured finally emerged. He'd told Anna Whitehead, his girlfriend, that he was on to the 'Big Job', a drugs deal worth over a million. A light plane was supposed to be flying a consignment of puff over from Belgium and landing it on a field near Rettendon. Anna told me he kept saying, 'I can't wait for this to go off. I'm going to give Carlton 20 or 30 grand out of it.' She said he seemed more excited about giving me 30 grand than making a nice few quid for himself. It all turned out to be a hoax. But it rang bells with me.

By then I'd met the mysterious Mick the Pilot, Micky Steele, at a party at a mate's snooker hall in Dagenham. He was with his missus and didn't have a lot to say to Tony or me. But later on, Tony said he'd got this big drugs deal on the boil and did I want to put some money in and get a share of the profits? I said I hadn't got the dough and wasn't interested anyway. It turned out that this time it was a genuine deal but the puff they bought turned out to be jank gear, a pile of rubbish. It went back to the dealers and they got their money back.

By now, almost on a daily basis, I could see Tony and Pat were on high-octane fuel, getting wild, doing the most ridiculous things. They were doing dangerous stuff like racing their Porsches up and down the A127 Southend arterial Road at 140mph after a night spent mainlining on pure cocaine. They were also jacking up on ketamin, nubane and shit like that. Tony wasn't a womaniser but he was shagging other birds all the time, partying, drug taking, and so on.

I remember one weekend I was trying to contact him, but couldn't get hold of him. He was off the phone. It was important so I went to his house in Chafford Hundred, and knocked on the door. I thought something had happened to him. The door opened and Craig Rolfe was there with Tony. Craig was out of it.

Tony was sitting on the edge of a chair laughing, hallucinating on something. I said, 'What the fuck's going on, Tony?'

He muttered, 'Oh nothing, mate.'

I could see by his eyes he was on something heavy. He was pulling down his shirt sleeve to hide something. I grabbed it and pulled it up again. I was staggered. He had about 30 recent injection marks along his arm. 'What the fuck are you doing, Tony?'

I think he was too ashamed to speak. He was on the precipice and hadn't a clue just how close disaster was.

The first puff deal had left a nasty taste in the mouth and Tony, Pat and Craig had got the raging hump with Micky Steele. To make matters worse, from what I heard, Micky was having a relationship with Pat's missus, Sarah. Pat and Micky had met in prison and had known each other a lot longer than Tony or Craig. So it was well out of order for Micky to be bedding Pat's wife, even though Pat was always out on the town, always with other women.

Pat was awesome. He was a big old boy with a big reputation and he'd looked after a few people in prison and was well respected. He knew Reggie Kray well from Whitemoor and had minded a gay boyfriend for him. Yes, Reg was as queer as Ron. Pat was a character and I liked him.

Micky got to hear that Pat knew about him and Sarah's

affair and was gunning for him. So,according to what I heard after the murders, Micky and his pals decided to do Pat and the others before they did them. Micky was very clever, very manipulative. He told Pat and Tony that there was a big drugs deal going down and they would wait for a planeload of gear to arrive. When it landed, they would rob the people, take the drugs, grab the money and pull off a right old coup.

The night they died, I was told, my three mates had gone down that country lane on a dummy run to get the lie of the land. It was all a scam. Their trust, or perhaps it was their greed, was rewarded with that terrible massacre that shook the Essex gangland scene to the core. I wasn't invited in on this deal, phoney or otherwise, thank God, because they knew I hadn't got cash to invest. But that night at the party when I'd had that bad, bad feeling, and suspected something heavy was about to go off, I'd pulled big Pat to one side and told him, 'Look, I love Tony like a brother. If anything happens to him, I'll hold you responsible. Look after him. Don't let me down.'

I saw them on the Friday before the murders when we had a drink at Berwick Manor, near Upminster. Their secretive attitude did nothing to lessen my fears for Tony's safety. They were whispering, furtive, and not their usual selves at all.

The night of the massacre, Tony, Pat and Craig, three grown men, three dangerous men, all professional criminals, went out without a weapon between them. Their mobile phones were all switched off. They were driven to snowy Workhouse Lane in Rettendon where Micky Steele's partner Jack Whomes was already hiding with a gun. Steele was in the back seat and got out, supposedly to have a piss. Once he was out, Whomes passed him a pump-action shotgun. He leaned in and opened fire. Rolfe died first, his skull blown away, his hands still gripping the steering wheel, his foot still on the brake. In a split-second, Tony, sitting beside Rolfe, also got it in the head. Then Pat was blasted in the chest, head and belly by both gunmen as he begged for his life.

When anyone you know dies suddenly, or violently, it sends a shock wave of nausea through your body that makes you physically sick. As the details of the triple murder emerged, as yet with the killers unknown, I was wracked with a mixture of dread, panic and anger that led to me shaking with rage.

The next morning, the police were round my house in Brentwood saying that I could be a suspect. I'd got a team of boys round me from my own firm looking after me and I was crying like a baby. No way, I said, not Tony. I told the cops, 'Let's get one thing clear. If you bad-mouth my pal, if you slag him off, you can fuck off out of here right now.'

One copper said, 'We only want to eliminate you from our enquiries, Carlton.'

I fumed, 'Eliminate me? He was the best fucking mate I ever had.'

He said, 'Well, right now you are the top of our suspects list.'

3

Ghosts

The weeks had dragged on since the Rettendon murders and I needed answers. I knew who might supply them. Bizarre as it sounds, I was prepared to place my faith in a medium, a spiritualist, in one last desperate attempt to calm the raging fury that was driving me insane day after day. I was paranoid with anxiety by now, fearful of the constant police surveillance, worried that every passing car, every motorbike might be carrying a hit-man who would finish off what Rettendon had started. I'd got up morning after morning, looked at myself in the mirror and said, 'What have you got yourself into?'

I hoped Shirley might help. I knew the police had used her with some success to solve crimes or find missing people and my mum swore by her powers. I wasn't sure, but my mind was so troubled by now, I drove to her home in Gants Hill and asked for a sitting. No names, no background, I just needed to know that whatever she told me was not tainted by anything she might have read or heard about in the papers or seen on the TV news. Just Joe Bloggs come for a consultation.

I wanted to make contact with a missing friend, I told her. What I heard in her parlour that afternoon shook me rigid. I was there for an hour-and-a-half as she sat holding pieces of gold I'd handed her at her request, a sort of lightning conductor to the afterworld, as she sought to make contact with Tony.

Her eyes glazed over. She seemed to have reached somebody, some spirit somewhere out there in the ether. I went cold, I got shivers down my spine, the hairs on my neck stood on end. Bearing in mind that she had no idea who I was and why I was there and, at that stage, knew little about the murders, she was uncanny.

She sniffed the air and said, 'I can smell aftershave ... does that mean anything?'

I told her I'd bought my pal a bottle of Hugo Boss aftershave for his birthday two or three weeks earlier.

'He's just died, hasn't he?' she said.

That hadn't taken a lot of working out, so I was still far from convinced that, eerie though it was, this wasn't just guesswork and a bit of gimmicky theatrics. She held my gold chain, rubbing it gently, and within minutes she had started crying uncontrollably. There was a weird aura in the room. She looked at me and said, 'You've lost someone very close to you, haven't you? Something terrible has happened.'

Now I was starting to take notice.

She lapsed almost into a trance as she went on, 'I've never seen so much violence, so much blood.' She knew that three people had died. She said they were angry. They didn't want to go. One of them, she said, was a close friend who wanted to make contact with me. She kept saying, 'Violence, pain, anger ...' They were trapped, she said, unable to move on to the next life because of the way they'd been killed. It could take a year before their souls could move on.

I needed to know who had killed them. 'Who did it? Do you know their names?' I pleaded, thinking this might be the route towards a speedy revenge.

She seemed to be looking into the distance. Then she said, 'I don't know, but I can see three men standing together looking up into the sky, pointing at a small plane. They are shouting, "You bastard, Mick, you bastard."' She could see a Range Rover, she could see a white van with men getting into it, she could see a motorbike. I was sitting across the room, a few feet away, with my jaw dropping, amazed, astounded at what I was hearing, but still cynical.

At that point, only a Range Rover featured in the murder scenario. No one – not me, not the police, not the families of those involved – knew anything about white vans or motorbikes, or pilots, features of the case which were only to become significant many, many months later.

I was telling myself, 'Get real, Carlton. How can she know these things.' To a down-to-earth East End boy, while all this was fascinating, mind-boggling even, she knew I was unconvinced. She said, 'To let you know I am telling you the truth, your friend has asked me to mention Suffolk.'

Well, you could have knocked me down with a feather. Just two weeks earlier, me and Tony and Pat and Craig, the whole firm, had all gone up to Suffolk by car to sort out a problem at one of the clubs where Tony handled the security where some local dealers were serving up drugs which were not 'approved' by Tony. The manager asked Tony to get up a heavy team to sort it. We got up two carloads, about eight of us altogether, all experienced lumps in the muscle game, and we planned to arrive by surprise, lock up the back doors of the club and trap the dealers inside so they couldn't run anywhere, then clean up the problem. A commando raid, in essence. We thought one of the doormen was in on the racket as well, so we needed to give him special attention. It was a big mess and needed heavy treatment. We were happy to help Tony out. None of us were averse to a decent ruck.

Some of us went in through the back doors and bolted them, the others went in through the front. If anyone ran out on seeing our firm swaggering in, then they'd be trapped like rats. But as it happened, someone had tipped the local dealers off and when we got there it was all quiet, like a village church. There wasn't a dealer to be seen. The local punters were quiet. They'd been scared shitless at the sight of eight fucking great bodybuilders up from the smoke and stayed in small groups very quietly. It all passed off peacefully but we knew the warning message would soon get through to anyone thinking of taking us on at any time. We just had a few drinks before heading home.

Now, there was no way this medium could have known anything about that. It wasn't something we'd have talked about outside the firm. It was never in the papers. Yes, she knew too much for it to be simply a lucky guess, a stab in the dark. I was getting goose pimples now.

'Your friend has told me to mention Suffolk so you'll know it's him talking to you,' she repeated.

I knew all right. I don't care if nobody else in the world believes me or not, I knew what I had heard and she couldn't fake that. I was taking a few notes on a pad. My hand was shaking, making my writing spindly, almost unreadable. I wish now I had tape-recorded it all so that I had a record of everything she said.

'Your friend is telling you not to take revenge, don't go after the people who did this yourself. He's saying they will take their own revenge in the fullness of time.' She went into a sort of hypnotic state again. 'I can see a small plane in the sky,' she said. 'Now it's burst into flames and is crashing down.'

'Is that their revenge?' I asked.

'Yes that's their revenge,' she said.

It got spookier. She was now looking at the photograph of a young girl stuck on the wall with sellotape. It was one of many cases in which people had asked for her help with finding missing children, or explaining sudden deaths, suicides or murders. There were faces of people who had all been involved in some sort of tragedy and the relatives had sought some desperate kind of emotional consolation through Shirley to help ease their pain and their grief. People like me, looking for answers.

Then there were the baffling cases where even hard-nosed policemen had gone to Shirley's parlour to ask for help. If hard-nosed police officers used her talents, she surely wasn't some sort of cruel charlatan preying on the vulnerable.

She broke off from our conversation about Tony and the Rettendon killings for a few minutes and indicated the picture of a pretty, blonde-haired schoolgirl whose photograph was sandwiched amid rows of others, but seemed somehow to catch the eye.

'Do you see her?' she asked.

There was no mistaking who she was talking about. This was a school photo, capturing a girl full of happiness, full of hope, but you knew that because it was on Shirley's wall, this was a picture full of sorrow, too.

'She's pointing at you,' said Shirley.

I said, 'What? What do you mean?' I was getting uncomfortable. The room had gone cold. This was reaching beyond the realms of credibility for me.

'You mustn't be nervous,' she said soothingly. 'She's got something to say to you. She's come out of the wall, she's manifested herself here in this room to pass on a message.'

I began to question the wisdom of carrying on. We'd gone far enough down this road for me to start doubting my sanity.

Then came the final bombshell. 'You lost some loved ones in the Zeebrugge ferry disaster, didn't you?' Shirley enquired.

Well, by now I was quaking. I *had* lost loved ones in the tragedy. But so few people, and certainly not a medium in Gants Hill, could have known.

I'd had an affair several years earlier with a girl who worked as a barmaid in one of the clubs where I worked as a doorman. I was married at the time and wasn't prepared to leave my wife. So it all fizzled out and we drifted apart. I was told months later that she was pregnant. I tried to contact her but she didn't want to know. No big deal at the time; I'd got plenty going on in the club scene, plenty more girls to bed, so I got on with things.

Then after the terrible Zeebrugge disaster was in the headlines day after day and people were gradually being identified, a mate of mine at the Penthouse Club called me over one night and said, 'You know that barmaid you had a fling with ... well, she was one of the victims. Her and her son both drowned.'

Her son, my son? I was dumbfounded. Could it really be true that she was now reaching out to me, trying to say something to me. It was unreal. I know I was in an emotionally vulnerable state at the time, but how do you explain something like that? 'How did the photo get on the wall?' I asked Shirley.

'The parents,' she said, 'the mother's parents came to me. They were looking for answers like hundreds of other grieving relatives after Zeebrugge. They live near here and someone suggested I might be able to help.'

Rather like me really. I'd only gone there because a relative, in this case my mum, had seen all my anger and frustration boiling over and thought it might bring some consolation. Consolation? It had blown my fucking mind.

The police were visiting me regularly then about the murders and the next time they came I showed them the notes of my curious consultation with Madame Shirley. The Old Bill would always come to me, not the other way round;

I didn't want to keep any meets with them, because, like I say, I had this dark suspicion in the back of my mind that they had killed Tony and the boys. A bit of criminal ethnic cleansing to get rid of a firm getting too big for its boots. I had no evidence, just a gut feeling. It was wrong, as it happens, but at that point in time it was a very real possibility to me and the most plausible explanation for the murders.

Nevertheless, I knew I had to tell them about that session with Shirley, how intense it all was, how she had been left drained by the experience, how I'd been left bewildered by it all. The cops sort of looked at me sideways, like I'd cracked up, blown it, taken leave of my senses. This wasn't something they could take back to the nick as evidence. Shirley had freaked me out. I can't pretend anything else. A big, strong, hard man like me came out of there a blubbering wreck. I wished I hadn't gone there. Too much was going on inside my head that I couldn't comprehend.

Anyway, when the detectives came again and I told them about the consultation, one of them jotted a few notes down as I read from the pad I'd taken to Shirley's. You could tell he wasn't that interested. They wanted more practical help. What they were trying to do then was to get me to draw people out, go to telephone boxes and ring people up, try to get them to say things about the murders which might provide some clues, names maybe, or a motive. They still had few leads and mouths were staying shut in Essex. So many people said the same thing: nobody much liked the Tucker firm — or The Essex Boys, as they were known — and they were running out of control and getting up the noses of a lot of people. Plenty would like to see them dead. Police and Customs files were bulging with information about big drug deals, rip-offs of other dealers, shootings, stabbings, and even a murder in which Tony, Pat and Craig were supposed to be involved.

I knew a different Tony Tucker. Great mate, soul mate really. We'd had so many good times in the last few years. I believed most of his money came from his successful security firm, supplying doormen for clubs and bars, and his health shops supplying body-building foods and accessories legally, steroids illegally. Sure, I knew he was a bit of a 'face' with big-time aspirations and some heavy underworld connections. But, to me, he was genuinely a really nice guy.

I could see things had been changing since he formed a criminal triumvirate with the other two and had started taking drugs like there was no tomorrow and getting involved in stuff he couldn't control. But he was still my greatest mate and I wasn't ready to hear people slagging him off now he was dead, or slagging him off ever, come to that.

The cops really didn't want to know about the messages from beyond. They were chasing their own theories. But the detective who'd taken notes that day about my visit to Shirley was to come up to me many months later and say, 'Carlton, when you told me about the white Transit van I shivered. We'd only just found out ourselves that the killers were probably picked up in a battered white Transit, but no one else outside the murder squad could have known.'

Another weird thing that happened after the murders was Tony's home at Fobbing getting spooked. His mate Andy was looking after the place because Anna wouldn't stay there, despite all the security lights and fencing and alarms and guard dogs. She was frightened for her life as well. So Andy was going there every day to feed the dogs and horses. He phoned me and said, 'Carl, something weird is going on.'

He'd gone there and found lights turned on that he'd switched off the night before, pictures turned upside down, dogs let out when they should be in. He phoned Anna but she hadn't been there. He told me, 'I'm petrified, I'm sure it's Tony trying to say something.'

I was glad that it wasn't just me having these weird experiences over Tony's death. The triple murders had sent shockwaves throughout Essex and East London and a lot of people were getting screwed up with a confused mixture of emotions.

All those strange happenings slowly changed my attitude and my beliefs about the afterlife, about religion. I've never been a religious man. How could I be, cutting up people, beating them with iron bars, kicking shit out of them for a job? I'm not religious now, but I've come to believe very strongly that there is an afterlife, that we have an aura we leave behind, that our lives are mapped out and when your time is up, that's it.

I remember lying on my bed night after night in the months following the murders saying to myself, 'Who are you? What's your purpose in life?' If you come on this earth as a gardener, you garden; if you are an artist, you paint beautiful things; if you're a musician, you write lovely symphonies. I was asking myself, 'What do you do, Carlton, to justify being here?' Was I good or was I evil? Or was I here as some sort of balancing weight between good and evil to make sure that the innocent people don't get hurt?

At 4.00am, my mind was questioning every aspect of the world I was living in, the craziness of it all, the lunacy of driving about in cars with people with guns, knives, drugs, gear. I couldn't believe I'd reached this point where I could put my kids, my babies, in such danger. I'd go into their bedrooms while they were asleep, look at them and say, 'I'm sorry, I'm so sorry.' I was full of fear for their future, so afraid that they might reap the grim rewards of my lifestyle.

One night, I was on the door at the Ministry of Sound nightclub in London – top place at the time – buzzing, and the manager came out of his office and said, 'Carl, there's a call for you.' It was 2.30am. What the fuck is this all about?

I picked up the phone. 'Hello, who's that?'

'It don't matter who we are, we're outside your house and we're going to kill your wife and kids and you can't do fuck all about it.'

I said, 'Oh yeah, really?'

The voice said, 'Yeah, really, we're going to break in now and do them.'

I slammed the phone down. If they'd said they were outside my house and given my address in Brentwood I'd have been in turmoil. I'd have been back down to Essex like a rocket on rails. So I reckoned it was a hoax, some sick wind-up.

I tried to ignore it. But the nagging fears wouldn't go away. I knew there were people out there who would, and could, commit such an atrocity to get at me. You don't work in the muscle game most of your life and not make enemies. I paced up and down getting more and more anxious. What if it's not a hoax? What if they get killed and I did nothing to stop it? A couple of the doormen offered to come back with me. I said no.

Finally, the anxiety was too much. I said to one of my most loyal doormen, Tony East, 'Come on, we're going to take a look.'

We drove at high speed through the breaking dawn, down the Elephant and Castle, the Old Kent Road then over the river and headed for Essex. It was 5.30am when we arrived outside the house. We drove quietly round the house, round the green, no one about. Not a soul. I stopped the car a little way away so I wouldn't wake anyone, tip-toed back and peered through the windows, saw the dog asleep, saw that everything was peaceful and breathed a sigh of relief. I didn't go in. My girlfriend Denny – my common-law wife, actually, and mother of my two girls, Jodie and Jamie – would have crapped herself. Instead, I got back in the car and headed off to London and finished the night's work. I never mentioned a word about my secret visit to Denny and the kids when I finally returned home at about 11.30am. But I couldn't have taken a chance, could never have lived with the guilt if they had been harmed in any way.

In my world, anything could happen and often did. I was in a hard, brutal environment and I felt the need to apologise to them just in case it ever happened again. But in the end, I decided it was best left unsaid. It would have probably caused more fear than reassurance.

I don't live with Denny and the kids any more and part of the reason is that I don't want them ever to suffer for something that I do, or have done in the past. I still see them, still love them, but my kind of world is not for wives and kids. If some bastard comes through the door with a loaded shotgun looking for me, I have to make sure they aren't in the way. I'm not afraid of dying but I'm very afraid of my family getting hurt. Whatever happens, I won't forget the people who matter.

I've been in and out of relationships but I've always looked after my kids, I've never left anyone wanting and I've never taken what's not mine. I've had a lot of money through my hands. I could be living in a villa on the Costa del Sol if I'd been more sensible. But everything I've had I've spunked away. I've done the F-plan big time – I've fought, I've fucked and I've fed. Now I'm walking away from all that. I can handle the danger to myself, it goes with the territory. My kids can't be expected to carry that burden. They deserve more.

4

Door Wars

Big Lew dropped the troublemaker with a pile-driver of a right-hander. He was unconscious before he hit the deck. And he lay there flat on his back for the next ten minutes with a silly grin on his face like he was tucked up in bed in a four-star hotel. That was the way Big Lew did things. Two warnings and you're out. Knocked out. But don't get me wrong, Lew was no hulking brute who liked thumping people for the hell of it. In fact, he was probably the best club doorman I ever knew. A proper gent of the old school. Respected throughout the industry as hard, fair and effective.

The night he was forced to pole-axe the half-pissed geezer outside a Dagenham nightspot he was provoked by a tirade of abuse and threats that would have challenged the patience of a saint. In the end, he had no alternative. The bloke had come looking for trouble, and he got it. Lew had seen dozens of similar chancers take him on. Not one had ever succeeded. And no one got through the door when he said no. What was different about the 22-stone Northerner was that he had no malice whatsoever in what he did. He was old-fashioned muscle – smart suit and dicky-bow, out to stop trouble, not start it. A true mark of his style was that after he'd smacked the lippy bloke at the club, he checked that he was not seriously hurt, then organised a cab to take him home knowing that when he woke up he'd have a headache he'd never forget as a souvenir of his meeting with the big fella and a reminder not to be so stupid again.

That was the way it was done when I first got into the muscle business. A doorman had a sort of sinister charisma that carried a lot of respect. The drug explosion of the Eighties changed all that. It became more difficult, dangerous and dirty. The security industry, from bouncers and doormen to celebrity bodyguards and gangland minders, grew into a massive business turning over hundreds of millions of pounds a year, in both the straight and black economy. It made sure I was never out of work.

I reckon my firm of heavies was about the best in the business and at our peak we were involved in security at many of the top clubs in town. We were muscle for hire, at a price. And we were fucking good at what we did.

There had always been plenty of muscle around in the East End where I was brought up and, yes, I did admire gangs like the Krays and Richardsons. They had their hard men like Freddie Foreman and Frankie Fraser, their own little armies from generals down to foot soldiers, crude but effective fighting forces. One old-time villain once said to me, 'You are only as strong as the people around you.' I founded my firm on that basis. Total loyalty expected all of the time. It doesn't matter who you are, you needed that protection around you if you were to succeed in the jungle that the security business became.

I pulled together a team from all different parts of London, all nationalities. Previously, the North, South, East and West had ruled their own patch, provided their own heavies. The territories were jealously protected. A big night was covering a door where 200 or 300 people turned up for a Saturday night disco. Then, in the Eighties the rave scene swept Britain with tens of thousands of people turning up at illicit venues and dancing all night to acid house music. These so-called summers of love brought with them the new phenomenon of Ecstasy pills and vast new profits for dealers and drug smugglers. Yes, I had my snout in the drugs trough as well, but it had seemed so innocent to start with. I never imagined all the grief that was to follow with so many deaths of young kids and so much vicious gang warfare. We began to find that muscle wasn't being hired for the benefit of the youngsters but to protect the millions of pounds the organisers were raking in. It started to get very sour.

Celebrity bodyguards had become all the rage. Muscle was in demand for people like Madonna on her famous jogs in Hyde Park, for film and pop idols who feared for their safety. Showbusiness had been shaken by the murder of John Lennon in a New York street. Who could blame the stars for wanting a heavy in tow to look after their interests? The problem was highlighted again and again with attacks on George Harrison in his home and the murder of Jill Dando on her doorstep, for no other reason than they happened to be famous. Muscle became a necessity, not a luxury. People were becoming scared with just cause. When was the next publicity-seeking nutter going to make a name for himself? When was some evil stalker going to drive someone mad with worry?

People like me, and firms like mine, provided a sort of balance of power, straddling a line somewhere between gangland and showbiz, a bit like the Kray mob in its heyday, I suppose. We took on the jobs the coppers didn't want to know about. People were getting rich out of the drugs boom, turf wars were breaking out and people like me were being asked to do the dirty work. Knifings, beatings, even murders were happening around clubland and the Government and the police were getting worried. That deadly concoction of power and money was seeing certain people running out of control and it was time for a severe shake-up of the security industry. So in came compulsory registration and training in the early Nineties. My certificate shows that I passed my City of Westminster door supervisor training course in March 1995 at the Ilford Health and Fitness Centre. I became registered security operator 000115. Without that 'licence' I might never work again. It was, in many ways, the beginning of the end for the muscle game as I knew it. It gave councils who license clubs and the police who monitor them the opportunity to boot out people they regarded as undesirables – thugs and gangsters, in other words. It was clean-up time in clubland.

Unfortunately, the new restrictions often left a bunch of complete amateurs doing the doors and internal security. I know of clubs being covered by security staff who, by day, were painters and decorators, electricians, van drivers, whatever, and club doormen by night. Good luck to them, but I think it's dangerous.

OK, they go down the gym and get a badge to say they are trained security men but what they lack is street knowledge. They need to know a 'face' if he turns up, they need to know the dealers, they need to know the pimps and the prostitutes. You need to have done your homework, like a cabbie needs his 'knowledge' to survive.

It was for that reason my firm employed doormen from all over London, black and white. Wherever a job came up, I could call on someone who'd got his ear to the ground, knew the local scene, who were the possible troublemakers, what was going on between different people, would there be needle if certain people were in the club together. That's what the bosses paid their money for. People like Big Lew. That's not what they're getting a lot of the time now.

A lot of the new security blokes are working for peanuts. And you know what they say – if you pay peanuts, you get monkeys. A lot are just topping up another wage, moonlighting, looking for a little bit of glamour among the bright lights. In our heyday, me and all of my firm were full-time professionals. We commanded good money. I was taking home £50 a night nearly 20 years ago. If I did four nights on the door, it was £200 in the bin. Bloody good money. The better you were, the bigger your reputation, the more you could get. Good doormen were becoming mini-celebrities in their own right. Now, a few big firms have got hold of the security market, employing hundreds of part-timers for about £30 a time. That's all very well, but if the job is a big rock concert or something with 20,000 people and things threaten to kick off you've got to know what you are doing. You pick up a sixth sense about dangerous situations. You've got to know how to control, how to talk to people without inflaming the situation. The top boys have got it, the amateurs very rarely.

If it's a bodyguard you need, I'm your man. I've done a lot of minding jobs over the years and they've all been successful. Well, everyone's still alive and no one's been robbed, so I reckon I can call that successful. I like to combine a bit of research, a bit of experience and a lot of intuition with a spot of animal cunning. It's my nature to be a bit jumpy, always on edge, looking for possible bother. But that's better than being complacent and waiting for trouble to find me. When I've stood in clubs with my mate Nigel Benn, you get a lot of people wanting to come up and shake his hand. They want to be seen with a celebrity, get a little bit of reflected glory. Then you might see someone who just doesn't look right. You get suspicious right away. He looks a bit weird. He's moving forward, his hand is going into his pocket ... to me there's no argument. Move in, grab him, get him up against a wall, let's have his hand out of his pocket to see what he's got. It could be a blade. On the other hand he might just have been scratching his bollocks. It doesn't matter to me. I've got to know. I'm in the protection business and I can't take chances or waste vital seconds. If the bloke turns out to be a normal clubber just out having a good night out, that's too bad. A split-second's delay and your celebrity could be lying on the floor with a knife in his guts.

I said to Nigel over and over again not to let people get too close. But he's a great bloke who is more than happy to glad-hand someone if they want to meet him. You can't cover everyone all the time, but you can even the odds by keeping one jump ahead. The weirdos out there looking for notoriety by attacking someone famous are a chilling fact of life today.

Some of the lumps I've seen doing security work these days don't seem to know their arse from a bank holiday. The key is always on the door. That's where you stop the trouble. Control the door properly and you run a safe club. It's no good trying to root out every tin-pot drug-dealer going in for the night. Make no mistake, drugs and clubbing go hand in glove. Who am I to say whether someone should or should not snort a line of Charlie off the toilet seat or pop a couple of Ecstasy tablets? They are going to do it anyway. But where you've got drug dealers, you've got drug wars. I've seen some vicious in-fighting between rival dealers. That's why you need experienced boys on your firm who know who's who, know when the opposition move in, know when someone's likely to pull a blade. That's why my outfit was built up from switched-on guys from all over London. I always had every corner covered.

If we'd got a black problem at a club for whatever reason, we'd put a black team of doormen in to make sure we didn't get accused of being racist and people shouting, 'You've only knocked us back because we're black,' and that sort of thing. If we'd got a white problem, we'd put a white team in to sort it. I think we were the first multi-racial, multi-cultural firm of heavies in London. I was happy with that. I'd been brought up in the East End and went to school with black kids, never felt any animosity towards any black people, always worked with them great over the years. I picked the hardest of the white guys and the hardest of the black guys, making us one of the most powerful firms in the muscle business.

One of my West Indian doormen said once, 'Carlton, you're way ahead of your time in race relations ... you should be in the government.'

I wasn't exactly beating a path to Downing Street, but I was proud of the respect I was getting. It was returned tenfold.

At the same time, there were plenty of small firms out there with bad attitudes, along the lines of 'We're the guv'nors round here.' Because we represented the best from both worlds, we became stronger. My firm, at its peak, was about 30-handed. That's a lot of mean muscle. And we were in demand. 'Come in and clean up our club, we've got problems. We'll pay good money.' The calls came in one after another.

We were right on the case. We'd do the business. Then we'd find ourselves in a Catch 22 situation. You've cleaned up the trouble and they don't want you any more. They get a bit frightened of you and your little army. They are paying you over the odds because they know you are good. But they don't want to say, 'Sorry, we don't need you any more because you are too expensive and we no longer have a problem,' so you find £30-a-night doormen suddenly appearing who haven't a clue and you get called into the manager's office to be told, 'Oh, we've had the police in and they say they don't want gangsters on the door so we'll have to let you go.' What can you do but move on? For every door that closes another one opens.

The drug bosses were themselves hiring muscle to protect their lucrative pickings in clubland. So much money was being made, especially from the dance drugs like E, speed and coke, that criminals were robbing each other all the time. I didn't know until after Tony Tucker's death that he, Pat Tate and Craig Rolfe were supposed to be into robbing other villains in a big way. Drugs barons were hiring muscle to protect their ever-growing empires. The rip-off firms reasoned that it was pointless taking the risks of illegal importation and distribution when they could just go along and take drugs and cash from other villains. After all, what crooks could go to the cops and say, 'Excuse me, officer, but I've just been robbed of £100,000 worth of drug money.' So the big-time dealers were bringing in hired help. This was dangerous territory. You had to sit around in offices, rooms, warehouses, pub car parks, wherever a trade was going down. You take a look at the other people there. They're looking at you. No one says much. You think, What the fuck is going on? Are we here for a trade or is someone about to rip us off? You can shit yourself expecting some cunt to pull out a gun and let fire. But a bit of fear is healthy, it makes you a survivor. Without fear, you end up dead. But never, never show it. I've been in situations where I've been surrounded by ten fucking great minders looking after a deal. But I've never let my guard down. Drop it once and you're finished, you're on the ropes.

I steer clear of heavy stuff these days. Been there, done that, got the scars. Everyone in the game has taken a bit of a kick in the bollocks. The old-style hard men are being put out to grass. The work isn't there any more. Whether it's the police, the public, society in general, I don't know, but if you've got a bit of form these days, you don't get the good door jobs where the money is made. But get a situation where a problem crops up that the police don't want to get involved in, they'll soon let you back in to clean up a mess. And they'll turn a blind eye if a few people get bashed. They don't want to be in there with loads of paperwork and court cases when we can do the job our way. Everybody wins. We get some work back, the club gets straightened and the cops get a mess on their doorstep cleaned up without lifting a finger. That's the law of the street. There has to be a balance of power, and it's often people like me who control it.

We had that kind of situation at the Ministry of Sound nightclub at the Elephant and Castle in South London run by Lord Palumbo's son, James. It was the 'in' place to be seen. The rave scene moving upmarket, celebrities clamouring to be seen there, kids flocking from all over Britain to dance the night away. It was really taking off big time while we were running the Paradise Club in Islington. Then one of the Ministry's security guys, whom I knew as Northern Robbie, came to me and said, 'Carl, I want you to get a top team up. We've got all sorts of problems that need sorting.'

That's the way it was done, word of mouth, reputation.

This, in muscle terms, was the big one and I wanted it. Robbie hinted at dodgy doormen, money going missing, bullying of punters, all sorts. I said, 'Right, we'll take it on.' I knew it was well within our capabilities. Basically, it was a clean-up job and I'd got the boys to do it.

We had a meeting with the Ministry of Sound bosses to get a briefing on what needed to be done. In short, root out the old security firm, except for a couple of doormen considered OK, and get the place hassle-free again.

I wasn't happy, though, with any of the old security firm staying. I could only see them as potential enemies. They would still have contact with the sacked staff and that could prove dangerous. My fears were quickly confirmed when the Ministry threw a first-year anniversary party at which clubbers would be dancing round the clock, a full 24-hour rave-up. I needed to rotate my boys so that we were adequately covered until the very end. I had doormen coming in, doing a shift, going home for a sleep, then coming back for another session.

I was sitting in the security office when I clocked some familiar faces slipping in – the sacked door staff. I thought, This isn't right. Something's going on. They were being given the nod by their ex-buddies I'd been told I must keep on. The 'old pals' act.

I sensed something was going on that wasn't good for us, that somehow we were being set up, though I didn't know quite how. But I knew one fucking way to find out. I'd got only about three or four of my own boys on duty because the others were on breaks or having a meal. I'd seen one of the former doormen sneak in and he was talking to the club manager. Something was going to kick off, I was certain.

Because of my suspicions, I'd gone to work prepared for some aggro. I'd taken a bag of tools in a plastic holdall, a couple of knives, some coshes, baseball bats, anything useful. I gabbed a sheath knife and ran through the club with it in my hand. The ex-doorman saw me coming and suddenly his arse was in the air and he was trying to keep away from me. Then I clocked a couple of my top boys coming down behind me who I thought had gone home. The other firm had got the manager surrounded by now in a back alley at the rear of the club. He was in trouble. We weren't going to have any shit. This was our big challenge and how we handled this would make or break our reputations for years to come.

So me, black Gary, Tony and two or three others stood there tooled up and ready for action. I said 'Gary, this is going to go off here. They are all around us. What do you want to do?' I needn't have asked. He was ready for action. Right, we agreed, whoever came at us first, we'd chook them up. That was our code for knifing the bastards, cutting them up. Rearranging people's faces was an occupational hazard in our game, so we weren't going to be bothered by a bit of spilt blood. We stood with our backs against the wall so no one could get behind us and attack from the rear. I shouted, 'Come on then, who's first?'

We were well outnumbered but I knew my boys were capable of taking them on two or three to one. They were the best in the business.

We then found ourselves in a tense stand-off. Who would

crack first? Who would strike the first blow? The atmosphere was electric. No one moved. Their top guy looked for a second or two like he was about to steam in. We'd agreed that if he made a move, we'd try to take him out first, kill him if necessary, to force the others to back off. He saw three sets of hard eyes watching his every move. Then he turned and walked away. We'd called their bluff. The others followed in ones and twos and sloped off into the night.

One wrong move, one wrong word, and we might have had a bloodbath that night. But I think the other mob could see that they were up against three mates who would die for each other before they would ever turn their backs on trouble. It was an important victory for us in reinforcing our authority on the Ministry of Sound security. And important for our reputation as top guns in the muscle business.

It took us another couple of weeks to clean the place up, to get rid of those scumbags causing aggravation and get the door sorted and security running smoothly. Then, as so often happened when the waters quietened, the club tried to let us go. Thanks a lot and on your bike.

They were talking about bringing in a two-bob security firm for about £50 a night. I knew they'd soon be in trouble again if they did. The club was now high-profile, getting mentions in the press, and sooner or later would become a possible magnet for drug-dealers. I told them security was a job for professionals and if they lost their grip on it now, they would be in deep shit in no time at all. All the signs were there. I'd seen it before at other clubs. I promised them that my firm could hold it together. We did. For the next two years.

To say it was plain sailing would be a joke. The security business tends to be about as smooth as the North Atlantic in a force ten gale. That's the nature of the beast. At one club I worked at, I knew things weren't right when one of the staff – or I assumed he was staff, because he was at the interview where I got the job – came up to me one night and said, 'See that geezer over there? He's a drug-dealer. Chuck him out.' So I did.

I assumed it had been an official order from the management. Then the same guy came up and said, 'There's another over there, and another one there serving up drugs.'

I said, 'Hold on a minute, mate, who exactly are you?'

He said, 'Oh, er, I work here.'

'As what?' I wanted to know. He was looking flustered. I knew he wasn't right.

He lowered his voice so no one could hear. 'I'll tell you what,' he said. 'For every dealer you chuck out for me I'll give you a tenner.'

'You what?' I said. 'Get in the manager's office, cunt, and we'll sort this out.'

I expected the manager to blow his lid. But his response just served to thicken the plot. Instead of sacking the geezer on the spot, he said, 'Look, Carlton, it's like this. We've got a couple of our own people working drugs here and we want the opposition out of the way.'

By implication, he was saying that senior management at the club were getting a rake-off from actively promoting drug-dealing and giving the pushers protection. As I've said, I'm not naïve about drugs and I knew the club scene was awash with gear. The rave scene equalled kids on Ecstasy.

The smart West End clubs all had pet cocaine dealers who appeared to ply their trade without too much interference. You'd be a fool not to acknowledge that the drug culture in Britain is a fact of life that we have to accept. It's not going to go away. People taking social drugs by choice is not a problem to me.

I decided that this particular club's scam was a game that two could play. The following Friday, always a busy night with kids flocking in from all over the UK, I threw all the known dealers out. Every single one. There wasn't an E in the place. This place was drug dry. And the night was dead. The punters were there, the music was there, but nothing was happening. It was about as exciting as a WI whist drive.

'Where's so and so?' I was asked a dozen times. I knew he dealt Es and speed.

'Don't know,' I said.

'Then what about so and so?'

'Don't know.'

The night flopped disastrously.

The next day, I was called in by one of the anxious bosses – I can't name him for obvious reasons but, believe me, I know it – asking, 'What's going on? What are you up to?'

I told him, 'I'm getting rid of the dealers, cleaning the club up, kicking them all out.'

He said, 'But everyone went home early last night.'

'Yes,' I said, 'I know.' I knew, and certain people at the club knew, that drugs were as important, if not more important, than the music and drink on rave nights. Without the dealers, the club would die a death in weeks.

There was a bit of whispering between certain people. Then the guy who'd called me in said, 'Look, we can sort this. What if we give you a bit of rent money?'

Rent money? So this was the score. They wanted to bung me a nice backhander each week to turn a blind eye to the activities of their own pet dealers and boot out anyone who looked like opposition. I knew we were talking tens of thousands of pounds a week being turned over in the Ecstasy trade at clubs all over the country. I know I should have said, 'Bollocks, stuff it,' but I'm no saint and you've got to earn a crust when you can. I didn't have a problem with Ecstasy. I gave them the nod.

'OK, you're in on the deal.'

From that day on, I got a tasty bonus every week for allowing only management-approved dealers to operate in the club. I'm sure the owners didn't know what was happening, but certain key members of staff were involved in a massive drugs ring serving up pills to kids week after week to lure them into the club.

The money, always in used readies, never came directly from anyone I could identify. It was just there regular as clockwork delivered in a brown envelope by a third party who probably had no idea he was paying me protection money. In my own mind, I was telling myself that as Ecstasy was such an inescapable fact of life on the club scene, at least it was better that we partly controlled it to make sure only good gear was being peddled and to stop the scaggy bastards who were starting to bring dangerous crap into the country. I didn't want any Ecstasy deaths or injuries on my conscience.

There was also the matter of self-interest. If the shit did ever hit the fan over the E trade, they'd soon lay the blame at the door of the security department.

The management always denied that drugs were rife at that particular club. They would, wouldn't they? But I knew exactly how much it thrived under the vigilant eyes of people like me, getting my regular kickback by making sure business was brisk. Hundreds of kids were dropping Es every week, at about £20 a time, and dancing the night away in happyland. You can't tell me it was the mineral water that gave them the buzz!

Although I knew exactly what was going on, I didn't want to be seen to be part of it. No moral problem, just needed to stay a bit smart. I never knew quite where my backhander came from and I usually got a pal to pick up the cash for me to keep a bit of distance between me and the dealers and to make sure my fingerprints were never on the envelope. I knew the tame dealers, of course, but I tried never to speak to them, or acknowledge them as anything other than ordinary clubgoers. I certainly wasn't in the business of saying, 'How are the sales of Ecstasy going, mate. I need a bonus to get the missus a new three-piece suite from DFS.' If the drugs squad came steaming through the door one night, I'd be standing there saying, 'Drugs? Haven't got a clue what you are talking about.' That would make me the scapegoat, of course, because as Head of Security I should have known. But lying was better than a long jail sentence for being part of a huge conspiracy to supply drugs.

Business boomed, packing in hundreds of people a night

with queues outside. The door became ever more important. Numbers had to be restricted to avert any possibility of a tragedy caused by overcrowding. Punters regularly offered £50 notes to jump the queues or slip in through the back doors. It was always a no-no. If we'd had a problem with too many kids packed in there, my name would come up. I was fronting the place and I was responsible. I had to turn down a fortune in bribes on the door but it was one thing I couldn't risk. I used to see the heaving masses in there some nights and wondered whether someone else wasn't working a little scam.

But getting back to my job at the Ministry, all good things must come to an end I suppose. They said they didn't want me as Head of Security any more and were trying an experiment where different blokes would be running the door – two weeks one person runs it, for two weeks another, then another. I was furious. I told the management geezers, 'Hold on, this is my fucking door. This is my team. These boys work for me and no one else.' They wanted to start the rotation system with a security guy I'd never seen before.

'Fuck off,' I said, 'I'm out of here.'

5

Bad Vibrations

The very same day that I stormed out of the Ministry of Sound in a huff, the place got robbed. An armed team went in there and got about £38,000 takings. I knew I was certain to get a tug from the Robbery Squad. It couldn't have looked worse for me. Hours after a bust-up in which I told them to go fuck themselves, the place was done over. Talk about motive, opportunity and inside information. If I hadn't got a watertight alibi – that I was at home asleep when it happened – I knew I was certain to get my collar felt and who could have blamed them? But blagging was never my game. I'd seen too many end up in Wormwood Scrubs.

The cops were soon satisfied that I was clean on this one and left me alone. They also pulled another of my firm, who had a bit of form for armed robbery, but they had to let him go as well. It was a heavy-duty job and whoever pulled it off had excellent inside knowledge of the club and the security there.

I'd left a couple of my firm behind when I charged out supervising the counting and bagging-up of the previous night's takings. Both men were threatened with shooters and handcuffed together by the robbers. It was a professional job and I heard a few names being bandied about as to who was behind it. I think it turned out to be an ex-employee who, like me, knew the ins and outs of the club and when the money would be nicely bagged up waiting for security to take it to the bank.

The next thing I heard was that the club had offered Lenny McLean, one of the hardest men in London, £500 a night to front the door and to stop me going back. I'd never met Lenny but his reputation was massive. I had mates in the underworld who knew him and they said he was awesome. But I was seriously pissed off. I wanted the door back and, even if this meant a war with Lenny McLean, I was going back to try to reclaim my territory.

Through a mate, quite a well-known figure in gangland, we arranged a meet to sort things out, or at least see how the land lay. Where else could the meet be but in a jail? Not exactly my favourite venue but my mate had been going to meet a friend in Ford Open and Lenny had been doing a bit of debt-collecting for the same geezer and needed to talk to him. So inside the nick it was.

We all met up at Ford on a grey afternoon, pissing with rain, and sat round a table to talk door wars. My mate Jimmy introduced us.

'Lenny, this is Carlton. Carlton, this is Lenny.'

The handshake was like a fucking vice. He turned out to be a proper geezer who was willing to listen to my proposition that if he took the door at the Ministry, I would pay him £400 a month to mark my cards. I reckoned I needed someone feeding me accurate information from inside the organisation so that I could prepare my move to reclaim the security slot. I wasn't talking protection money because I didn't need his protection. What I did want was my job back. I wanted to work with Lenny, not against him, to achieve that aim.

At the end of the day, the whole plot fell flat because Lenny told the Ministry he'd changed his mind and didn't want to front the door after all. So they brought in some other security firm instead. Not surprisingly, doormen started getting beaten up, and there was no respect any more. People were just turning up and pushing the doormen out of the way. So I got the phone call I'd been hoping for.

'Carlton, can you come back? People are taking the piss and it needs sorting again.'

I was up for it all right, but now it was on my terms. First of all, more money. Then I had a meeting with James Palumbo and shook hands on a deal that would put my firm back on front-line duty again. I liked James. We came from vastly different backgrounds but we talked the same language. So it was back to business in a couple of days and we started a massive shake-up of the security set-up just like we'd done before. We'd soon got things back under control and I thought this would see me installed as clubland's top doorman for a long, long time. But, as I've said, it's turbulent waters in that game and it wasn't long before I heard on the grapevine that a new outfit was about to make a move against me. A hard-case out of North London, whom I knew only as Micky, had partnered up with Lenny McLean and they were trying to grab the door behind my back.

I decided on a pre-emptive strike. I called Micky and asked him straight, 'Is that right you are trying to nick my door at the Ministry?'

He was a bit flustered. He knew I was in fighting mood.

'Er, you'd better talk to Lenny.'

By now I was furious. 'I'm fucking talking to you, cunt. Are you after my door?'

He repeated, 'You'll have to talk to Lenny.'

I shouted, 'I don't want to talk to Lenny. He's got fuck all to do with this. He's getting too old for it. If you want to take my door, then come down to the door on Saturday night, and bring Lenny with you if you like, and you try to take my fucking door.'

War had been declared. I got home that night and thought to myself, Have you gone mad? You've just picked a fight with two of the hardest bastards in London. But sod it, this was shit or bust and I was up for a battle.

That night, we went in tooled up with guns and knives and coshes to defend the door. If Lenny did turn up, we knew it would be serious. He was a big fucker who could break your neck with one hand. I didn't underestimate his power and I didn't want to get into a fight I couldn't win. In my eyes, I was facing the ultimate test of my street credibility. I decided, 'Fuck it ... if he comes at me, I'll shoot him. He's a fearsome 22-stone man and I'll say I did it in self-defence.'

No cunt was taking my door and the shooters and knives would be enough to see off all-comers. If James Palumbo knew what was brewing, he'd have crapped himself. I had a quick council of war with the boys. At least 20 had turned up, a small army of seriously hard men, ready to fight for our territory. If Micky and Lenny and their rival team turned up, I said, we'd go for them straight away, stab 'em, shoot 'em, chop 'em, do whatever had to be done to send the bastards packing.

We were all wound up like coiled springs as every car, every taxi, arrived at the club. The hours ticked away. The onslaught never happened. The take-over bid had been aborted for now. I was mightily relieved. A massive battle between London's top musclemen, and the casualties it might have produced, would not have looked good in the newspapers for anybody.

So it was back to more diplomatic means – in our language, Jimmy going along to Lenny McLean and laying it on the line.

'You've shook hands with Carlton on this and you are supposed to be looking out for him. What the fuck is going on?' For good measure, he added, 'Carlton is fucking furious. If you cross him, he'll shoot you.'

Lenny said he didn't want any grief and wasn't planning any moves to get the Ministry door. The atmosphere settled down again. But we always knew some fucker would be trying to make a move against us – it was probably the best door in London – when we least expected it. So I told the boys never to drop their guard. I wasn't sure about Lenny's motives. He'd let me down after shaking my hand, and taking my money, then gone behind my back when someone came along with a better offer.

I'd never back down to Lenny. If he ever came to take the door, he'd have to kill me. Or I'd kill him. I really would. But I didn't need the aggravation and, as a sort of peace gesture, I resumed paying him the £400-a-month drink to help keep the lid on things while I got on with the job at the Ministry for a few more months.

As the club flourished and the cash kept rolling in, I became quite pally with James Palumbo. He seemed to have a fascination with my lifestyle. We'd have meals together in Knightsbridge and he was always asking me about my background, my lifestyle, what criminals I knew, had I ever met the Krays? It was all a million miles from his privileged upbringing but there was a mutual respect between us. He recognised that I was my own man, always spoke my mind and didn't arse-lick round him like most of his toady employees. At the same time, I always sensed he was a little bit wary of me.

I'd hollered about cuts in security spending at various meetings when they were talking about spending ten grand a night for a celebrity DJ, to fly him in from America, do this, do that, waste money here, waste money there, but if I wanted an extra hour or two on security it was up in the air. I'd say to James Palumbo, 'You're fucking wrong.' The others would look horrified and say, 'You can't talk to him like that.'

I'd say, 'If I think he's talking like a cunt, I'll tell him he's talking like a cunt. End of story.'

I told them that if I run the door, then I run it my way. I didn't want anyone telling me how to stand, what to wear or how to talk. But that's what was happening. People were treading on my toes. The atmosphere was getting strained again. It was another power struggle on the boil.

Then came the day I knew I'd got a Judas on my firm. The management said, 'Look, Carlton, we want to keep your security people on, but we want to pay you £250 a week not to come to work.'

I was dumbstruck, insulted. They wanted to pay me to sit at home doing fuck all. Had I become that dangerous, that much of a liability, that they didn't want me on the premises any more? I thought, No, I'm not having this. This is my team and they work for me. If they work, I fucking work.

I refused to stay at home. I sensed there was a conspiracy going on to get rid of me altogether. And my fears were confirmed when a copper I knew told me my file had been pulled at New Scotland Yard. That meant only one thing –I was under observation. They were out to get me.

The cop, who I'd only just met, worked for the London Transport Police. He was a half-decent geezer and he'd got me a couple of things, like a nice pair of police-issue leather gloves, and we got on OK together. He made no secret about being a cop but whether he came into the club on official business or just as a punter I don't know. Anyway, I'd asked him once if he ever heard anything, if my name ever came up, to let me know.

One night he came in and said, 'I've got something to tell you. They are trying to set you up.'

I said, 'Oh, are they fucking really!'

Then one of the managers said he wanted to see me at a meeting in a Knightsbridge hotel the next day. When I got there, two of my so-called mates, part of my security team, were already sitting with him. The fact that they wouldn't look me in the eye told me all I needed to know. We were at a big table, all official, and they had notebooks in front of them. There was a notebook and pen for me.

I said, 'What's all this bollocks?'

I was told it was so we could all take notes. I lost my rag, I'm afraid.

'Notes?' I said. 'Notes, you soppy cunts ... we're all grown men here. Why do you want to take notes?'

'Well, what do you want to go? We'll give you £5,000.'

I said, 'No, I want ten grand.' Deal agreed and I walked out that weekend with a nice ten grand to follow. Half the doormen walked out with me. They were the loyal ones, the others were dogs. They should all have walked out with me.

My pay-off came in ten envelopes each containing £1,000. I told the loyal lads that if they couldn't find work, I'd pay them 'til they got sorted. I knew it was time to move on. I'd had my days at the Ministry, I'd had some good money. It was a no-win situation. My muscle was up for hire again and I was waiting for takers.

★   ★   ★

My next job was at the Site club in London's West End. Again, it was a clean-up mission. Dealers had infiltrated, staff were being threatened, tough treatment was needed.

Tough treatment it got. Nobody hurt, mind you, just people knowing where they weren't welcome and what would happen if they stuck their noses round the door again. The wrong faces never got past the door. Within a couple of weeks, we had it running sweet again.

Two months on and we got the usual crap. 'Oh, Carlton, the Old Bill have been in asking about you. They're not happy. We're putting CCTV cameras in to catch the dealers so we won't want you any more.'

So it was time to move on again. It happened all the time. We did the dirty work, we cleaned up the shit, we restored the reputation. People felt good again. Then all of a sudden they wanted you out. They said it was the police, I was too heavy, but I don't really know if that was the truth. I think sometimes I became a challenge. People knew I was a bit of a hard man. I'm not the hardest man in the world, but I am hard when it's necessary, and they were worried someone might try to take me on at the door just because of who I was. Some people love that sort of danger thing in clubs, pushing their luck with the bouncers to try to impress mates or girlfriends. It's a dangerous game they're playing. Especially with me.

Now I've moved right away from the club scene. It's all changed so much that my reputation now works against me. My kind of security work just isn't there any more – unless it's a mess, the police are happy to let us clean up behind their backs, where they don't want to get their hands dirty. I don't need that any more.

These days, I'm into heavy-duty debt-collecting, and we're never short of work. My associates, and good friends, Gary Stokes and Jimmy Coleman, are about the best in the business. They're proper geezers. We've known each other 20 years and we respect each other and love each other like brothers. We're not into tuppeny-ha'penny debt-collecting or repossessing poxy cars and washing machines. The stuff we handle involves big money. If someone has been stuffed on a business deal and can't get their money, they make one phonecall and we're on the case. They'll get their cash. We don't have failures. We'll take a third, or even a half, of what we get. It sounds a lot but these are usually debts that were never ever going to be paid. So paying half to us is better than having no money at all.

We don't need to advertise. That's not the way it's done. People who need us know where to find us. We get the call, and Gary goes to see someone; he's very well respected in the underworld and knows a lot of faces. Then we flop on the people who have welshed on some deal or other and we sit down and we say, 'Right, we're the partners behind the scenes. You're dealing with us now. We've put 50 lumps into this and we want our money.'

They usually find the money real quick. We've just recovered £90,000 for an Asian businessman, a straight guy, who put up the cash through a third party to bring a legitimate consignment of drink in from Spain. Nothing hookey. But the people he gave the money to thought he was dodgy and they decided to rump his arse and keep the 90 grand. They came up with all sorts of dodgy excuses and iffy paperwork, but no booze. They gave the bloke a load of shit 'til he got so pissed off he called us in.

We had a meet with the bloke behind the scam, a real-life Arthur Daley character, in a pub garden. We were waiting discreetly inside the boozer with the Asian fella waiting for the welsher to arrive. The geezer was sat at a table in the beer garden. I went out and walked past him. Didn't say anything, just walked past, then round the car park, walked all round checking he hadn't got a back-up team or Old Bill hanging round. We clocked each other but nothing was said. We said to the Asian guy, 'He's outside, go and talk to him and call us out in five minutes. Tell him the people who put the money up for the deal are inside the bar and want to meet you. Tell him we're in this for big bucks and we need it sorted straight away.'

Well, the geezer was straight on his mobile phone to Spain speaking to the people where the lorry-load of booze was supposed to have gone missing. Later on, he pulled us aside and said, 'Look, I didn't realise who I was dealing with. But, honestly, on my babies' lives, I'm not a liar. I don't know what's happened.'

As soon as someone says he's not a liar, then you know he's a liar. The money was paid in a couple of weeks.

We do the business properly. No thuggery, no violence, unless it's absolutely necessary. We go out in smart suits and ties and turn up looking like kosher business people. But they can see that behind the £1,000 suits and £20,000 Rolex watches they are dealing with real muscle. We're troubleshooters now, no one fucks with us. We are a heavy-duty, tight-knit little firm that gets results. If you take on one, you've got to take us all. We're the invisible men who appear out of the shadows to get people's money back. If someone puts up a name to try to scare us off, like, 'I know so and so from such and such a firm,' it doesn't work. We know people all over in the muscle game – North, South, East, West, even up in Scotland, so we call their bluff. We do what we have to do. That's the real world of muscle today. Being a doorman isn't muscle any more. Nowadays, you can be a fireman or mini-cab driver during the day and a bouncer at night.

We are a necessary evil in today's world. A lot of people get ripped off for a lot of money, some straight, some criminal. They can't get their money back through the courts or through legitimate debt-collection agencies. They are just told to fuck off. So we step in to even the score. Nobody is ever going to tell us to fuck off. OK, it may be fear that gets results, but we succeed where others fail and there's a lot of people out there who are very grateful for that.

We succeed on our reputation as much as our tactics. We're all getting on a bit, all in our forties, but we are still all well known in the right circles. Gary's dad did 15 years inside and his family is highly respected. Jimmy's got form for some legendary acts of gangland violence and is very much respected. I've got a bit of form, for a bit of actual bodily harm, a bit of drugs and what have you, and my reputation as hard muscle still holds good, all over London and Essex. I mean, you wouldn't mess with us, would you?

We always try to settle matters on neutral territory. We're all family men, we've got wives, ex-wives, girlfriends and kids so we never take our problems to someone's house. We'd never turn up mob-handed on someone's doorstep frightening women and children. It's not their fault the old man has got a problem. We'll deal with that in a bar, a pub car park, anywhere we can check out in advance to make sure it's not a trap. We make the meet, we choose the place, and if people play ball nobody gets hurt. We never raise our voices. We sit and we talk. That does people. Gary does most of the talking; no one can pull the wool over his eyes. I sit right beside him looking sinister. Another heavy will sit a few feet away just staring at the bloke. It's enough to make anyone shit themselves. It works. Job done, they pay up. I'm not saying we wouldn't get a bit noisier, a bit heavier, if someone didn't cough up. But that hasn't happened yet.

Gary has got a proper debt-collector's licence which covers his straight business. But, nowadays, we only handle substantial company debts, or personal debts where a lot of money is owed. There's no future in repossessing Joe Bloggs's Ford Mondeo or his wife's HP washing machine. The firms that do those jobs are dogs. They go out on a car repossession and phone the police in advance so they're covered. We don't need any help from anybody. I remember a couple of heavies coming to repossess a Granada Scorpio from Tony Tucker which he'd bought privately from a mate not knowing some finance was still owed. One of them tried literally to grab Tony and pull him out. Tony slammed the door on the geezer. What did he do? He phoned the police and tried to have Tony nicked for assault. Fucking pathetic.

It's the same with a lot of doormen now. They'll take you

in the back room to check you out, they'll maybe give you a slap, but you slap them back and what do they do? They call the Old Bill. They think they're policemen nowadays. They catch someone having a snort of coke in the toilet and instead of just kicking them out and confiscating the gear they're straight on to the drugs squad going for the brownie points.

The real muscle these days exists in the real underworld, hard-core gangland, the drug-minders, the bodyguards, the firms paid to hurt, maim and even kill. Contract muscle. In our world, you can make one phonecall and for as little as a grand you can have someone terminated and stuffed under a motorway bridge. That's not our game, but who's to say if the price was right, that we might just consider a hit or a serious bit of wounding?

There is a lot of thieving going on among rival gangs and they need muscle to look after their interests. If you've just been stuffed for £250,000 worth of cocaine and you know who has done it, you can't call in the Plod but you can organise a bit of muscle to sort it out. We are the quiet enforcers. I tell people, 'We are your insurance policy. We are your cover note. If you get fucked, we'll do the repair work like any other insurance company.' It's rough justice, but it's a very rough world out there. If you are in the underworld, if you are a drug-dealer, or a stolen car dealer, you are only as strong as the people around you. If a rival firm gets to know that the opposition has certain people around them, they'll soon back off. Our reputation is our guarantee.

We had a publican mate call us in once because he was getting heavy bother from a firm wanting protection money, wanting to sell him hookey booze, launder money, that sort of thing, really making his life a misery. So I got a little team up and all we did was go and sit in the bar, just sipping our drinks and chatting, for three or four days, and the word got out that we were minding for the licensee and the trouble stopped. Never saw the geezers again. They knew it wasn't worth taking us on for a few hundred pounds a month.

We've all been down different routes, me, Gary and Jimmy. We've all fought with decent people, we've all been fucked off over the years, used up by different people and we've learned lessons the hard way. Now we use our experience to help other people who've got problems, other people who've been fucked by someone and can't do anything about it. Now they know they can.

We've reached an age where our experience is our protection. We still get the odd kick in the bollocks but they can't hurt us any more. We're getting long in the tooth but we've grown strong in our ways, we're a solid firm standing back to back, blood brothers who care about each other, and we're not going to be hurt any more.

I'm not talking about the police. They are not our enemy. We don't invite trouble from Old Bill and we don't put ourselves on offer. That's stupid. If you drive past a copper in a 50-grand car and shout 'Wanker' out the window, you are putting pressure on yourself. If you go out on a job and start pulling out guns, bashing people about, terrorising people, that's the same sort of pressure. We don't need that any more. We still get a tug occasionally if some grass puts our name up but what we are doing now is our own form of policing in a very violent and dangerous area. In a way, we're being the good guys now, the Robin Hoods helping out people who've got a problem.

We've got a working relationship with a load of travellers in the area. They are very loyal people. Gary knows them really well. He can make one phonecall and have 50 proper travelling boys here within the hour, armed to the teeth and ready to go to war. They are the ultimate back-up, awesome muscle. They can go in and wipe an opposition firm out then disappear off the face of the earth. More so than us. We've got families, kids, homes and mortgages whereas the traveller boys have no ties and have connections the length and breadth of Britain where they can vanish to. They all know each other. They all stick together.

We've got a couple of young traveller lads in particular, in their twenties, very dangerous, good money-getters, who can help out if we've got a problem just about anywhere. If we want to find someone who's done a runner and we've got a vague inkling where they will be, they'll tell us, 'Yes, we've got someone there, leave it to us.' And before you know it, they've got him.

I remember a mate's son fighting a traveller boy once down in Kent. Proper boxing match, it's a big thing with them. They love a good scrap. So the traveller boy was backed up by dozens and dozens of his family, relatives from all over the country and my mate was worried that it might all kick off if the boy lost and could get really nasty. So he phoned me and said, 'Can you organise some support for my lad?'

I was on the blower for an hour. I called all my doormen,

various people I knew and told them, 'Be here at such and such a time. Never mind what for, just be here.'

So they all turned up at the meeting point, we piled into ten or fifteen cars and steamed down to Kent. The place went deathly quiet as we walked in like a fucking army, 30 big, strong bruisers, old enough and ugly enough to frighten Attila the Hun. Big fuckers, some of them up to 30 stone, huge lumps, muscle like you've never seen.

One of the travellers said to my mate, 'Fucking hell, are they with you?'

He said, 'Yeah, they're with me.'

We all sat down and watched the fight. It was a good, straight bout. My mate's lad won on points, and nobody kicked off. They'd got respect for the muscle we'd pulled in and the evening ended with handshakes all round as the travellers and my little firm enjoyed a nice few bevvies together. Again, we'd held the balance of power in a dodgy situation. It was just a little boxing match between two 16-year-old kids, but it could have been ugly. There were 500 people in the audience, rival firms, bad feeling, but because we'd turned up mob-handed we held the balance of power and we made sure there was no aggro. There was no way they could have taken us on, so those kids had their big night without it being messed up by some fucking great brawl. Good result.

If I use the word 'respect' a lot, it's because it's all-important in the world of muscle. You must have it or you don't survive. You must give it or you don't survive. But self-respect is the most important of all. I've lost a wife and two partners and three different homes through my lifestyle, staying out all night, sleeping around, getting involved in criminal stuff, but I've still got self-respect. I've had to start again from nothing three times, right from buying a kettle and a bed. But I have pride in my home; it may be a bolt-hole with a security spyhole, but I want my kids and my girlfriend to be proud of where I live. I want them to believe in me as a person, not see me as some hard-case without feelings.

I steer clear of drugs now. It's death, prison, wars. I've been there and I know. It's just about the biggest menace in Britain today. Drugs supply arms the world over, they support terrorism and brutality and I can't see a day when it will ever end. It changed the club scene for ever. It changed my life for ever. Drugs have penetrated every level of society. Our anti-drugs propaganda seems to be failing miserably. The situation out there is as bad as it's ever been. Most of the crime out there is kids nicking, burgling or robbing old ladies to get a wrap. Drugs take away respect for anyone, especially for yourself, and once respect has gone you're on the road to hell. Believe me, I've seen it. I've been down that path and so have some good friends who aren't around any more to tell the tale.

6

King of the Hooligans

J was about six years old when my dad first took me to Upton Park to watch West Ham play, perched on his shoulders, cheering on the lads for all I was worth. Marvellous, innocent childhood entertainment. Never did I dream that ten years later I'd be running amok on the terraces as one of the most feared soccer hooligans in Britain, targeted by the police, hated by rival fans, dreaded at every ground country-wide for the mayhem I caused.

I suppose I was first hooked on football, and especially West Ham, when I stood wide-eyed in Green Street, Forest Gate after West Ham won the FA cup in 1964 and watched the Hammers' open-top bus drive through the cheering crowds on their victory parade. I was up on Dad's shoulders for a better view of the conquering heroes, wearing West

Ham's claret and blue scarf and waving a rattle, and cheering away until I was hoarse. It was a magical day and Dad could see I'd got the West Ham bug.

He was a good old boy, an ex-merchant seaman who'd been twice round the world, then worked as an electrician, and had been a fanatical West Ham fan all his life. He was thrilled when I showed all the signs of being an equally avid supporter. He was always pleased to take me along to home games, then to a few away matches, and I loved it. We were mates. He'd always be there to lift me over the turnstiles, hoist me up on his shoulders, or find me a good spot in the front of the crowd where I'd get the best view of the game.

My mum comes from Bermondsey on the other side of the Thames, so her family always supported Millwall. So one week Dad would take me to West Ham, the next to a Millwall home game, plenty of variation, no animosity. But as I grew up and went on to grammar school, I couldn't support two teams. It wasn't done, especially two teams so close together. So I nailed my flag to the West Ham mast.

My schoolboy passion for the team grew into an all-consuming obsession. I lived, breathed and dreamed West Ham United. I started to bunk off school to watch them, then at 13 or 14 I joined up with a crowd who went to every game, home and away. At 16, I got to know the real hardcore supporters, including Vicky Dark, who became a well-known bank robber, and loads of other mates who not only shared a fixation with the Hammers, but a mania for violence. Sheer, pointless, exhibitionist violence that was often seen on TV newsreels and condemned in Parliament.

As impressionable teenagers, our big heroes were a hooligan gang known as the Mile End Firm, blokes in their twenties, grown men to us, who would cause aggravation by running mob-handed into the rival supporters' end, fighting, getting arrested, chanting their signature tune 'Mile End, Mile End'. I used to think, Fucking hell, they are the business, they're the chaps.

Then another firm came along – TBF, the Teddy Bunter Firm – and they were just as crazy. I was in complete awe of them and all I wanted to do was be as wild, as tough and as feared as them. So we started our apprenticeship in football terror. I wanted my own firm to outshine all the others. We started doing little tests to prove our bottle to each other, like running single-handed into a crowd of 50 rival supporters and kicking off. It was a mega buzz. At 16 years of age, fit, tough and fanatical, I set out to become the guv'nor of the rowdiest bunch of soccer hooligans of all time. And that's how the Inter-City Firm of West Ham supporters was born.

It was a name that sent a shudder through any club we were visiting and through the local constabulary. I wanted to be the boss. I wanted to be respected. I wanted to be feared. I can't pretend the violence didn't play a big part, because it did. I wasn't a violent kid away from football grounds, not a skinhead or anything, always looking for trouble. But put me at a West Ham game and I became an animal. I played soccer myself, I loved all sport, went out with girls, but it all took a back seat to my soccer mania and the thrill of conflict. I was a soldier, a tough marine, a commando, out there fighting for my team. I wanted the adulation of the fans, I wanted to be a name on the terraces. Top gun.

We started earning our stripes with a campaign of violence that shocked Britain. I remember on one occasion running into a pub in Coventry which was full of rival supporters, jumping up on a pool table, picking up the cues and hitting out, throwing the balls and fighting with everyone in there. We'd get through the turnstiles at places like Middlesbrough and Sheffield Wednesday and make a run for the opposition end. We'd go in, about 30 or 40 of us, fists flying, kicking out, using coshes, and we'd be heroes. We'd get pulled out by the police and frogmarched past the away supporters and they'd all be cheering and clapping. The football was becoming unimportant. The violence was all-consuming.

I was thrown out of game after game. But my standing among the West Ham supporters was getting higher and higher. I was somebody. West Ham weren't all that brilliant a lot of the time so I didn't miss a lot when I got the red card. I thought that if they haven't got the best footballers, then at least they've got the best fighters.

From random attacks and sporadic outbursts of violence, soccer hooliganism became more organised. It became part of our culture, big time, and it was attracting people from all walks of life. Not every hooligan is a brainless yobbo. Skilled people, professional people, get a buzz, too. Raids on rival fans became carefully planned; there was an underground network of contacts that kept you posted on what was going on. Firms were calling themselves names like the Headhunters and the Bushwackers and were all trying to outdo each other in the scale of violence.

Our name, the Inter-City Firm, came about when we started to travel to away games via inter-city expresses. We did this so that we didn't have to go on the specially organised soccer specials which were patrolled by the police and you had to go wherever they said. We didn't want that. We wanted to be able to get off the train when we wanted, roam about the town, spring the element of surprise on the opposition and do the maximum damage.

A soap firm was doing a special travel offer at the time — two adults buy a ticket and two children go free. So we used to get the older people on the firm to act as the parents and say the younger kids were only 14 or something then we'd all chip in with the fare money and so we were getting to away games really, really cheap. And the bonus was that we were able to steer clear of waiting Old Bill at the other end and storm in like an invading army from any direction.

Our numbers were growing all the time – 30, 40, 50, we were becoming a formidable firm. Then we sussed out the student rail cards and started using them to buy cheap tickets. We were travelling all over the country, as far as Liverpool and Newcastle. But the West Ham bovver boys didn't yet have a big name up North. We set out to change all that. We wanted to be the best organised gang of soccer thugs in the country.

My mate Brett came up with the Inter-City name, just for a joke at first. He made up stickers with the inter-city logo scrawled on them, which we left everywhere. It said,

'Congratulations, you've just met the ICF'. Then we had a couple of rows with the opposition and two of the geezers got knocked out. We left them on the deck with the ICF stickers on their heads. The name stuck.

Our reputation for brutality and balls grew and grew, and I loved it. The papers picked up on it and soon we were front-page news as the nastiest bunch of hooligans in Britain. But we had some serious opposition as rival firms tooled up with more and more dangerous weapons.

On one raid up North to take on Newcastle's boldest, we arrived early and started on the booze in the home side's local pub called The Magpies. We'd had a skinful by match time and were were fired up for trouble. We got in OK and were put in the away supporters pen segregated from the Geordies by a wire fence. It was an unbelievable atmosphere. All of a sudden, the Geordie boys started throwing darts and sharpened coins over at us. One dart went so close I felt it brush my ear. That onslaught was followed, to everyone's amazement, by a petrol bomb being lobbed through the air in our direction. It whooshed like Halley's Comet, a great ball of fire heading straight at us. I don't know how they'd got it in the ground but now we'd got it coming our way. We were penned in pretty tight but we all managed to dive out of the way. One West Ham lad didn't quite get clear and had his cord trousers set alight, and one or two others got petrol burns. Nasty stuff by any standards. I jumped on the screaming lad who was on fire and rolled him over and over to put out the flames. He was OK, luckily, but he could have been scarred for life.

The railways and the law enforcement agencies – the police, the railway police, club security staff – tried to stop us travelling away by making tickets first-class only. So we travelled first-class. If we got banned from the trains altogether, we'd go by car or by coach, any way we could to get there. We'd meet up in the Britannia Arms, Plaistow, our battle HQ, on a Friday night and hold a council of war to plan the next day's tactics. We had little hooligan platoons from all areas of East London – the Towners and Snipers from Canning Town; the Chads from Chadwell Heath; the Brits, us lot from the Britannia, about 30 of us who did the planning. Everybody knew each other by name. Strangers weren't welcome. When you got on the train the next day, you knew exactly who was there. You knew they were safe. My ambition was always to be up front, leading the attacks, being mad, getting the big reputation. I did crazy things to get recognition. I'd run into a hostile end on my own and have a barney. Or I'd go in with a small, select team and hurt a few people. We'd run through the crowds singing West Ham chants. A path would clear and people would point and shout and say, 'There they are, the ICF.' To me, it was like popstar adulation.

On one visit to one of our arch enemies, Chelsea, I had been expecting the troops to be following me loyally into battle in The Shed. But somehow they didn't seem up for it. One by one they were slipping off for a piss, or buying a hamburger or getting a drink. By the time we got to the segregation fence there was only one geezer behind me. It kicked off when the Chelsea boys saw we were only two-handed. Suddenly, they're all trying to get me, digging and kicking and punching. I thought, I've got to get the fuck out of here. My shirt was ripped, my jeans pocket torn off and the Chelsea mob were trying to drag me over the fence. Then some more of my boys turned up and they grabbed my legs. So there I was, stuck on the fence like a fucking great Christmas cracker being pulled from both ends and about to explode. I got pulled over, then I got pulled back. This went on for about five minutes. I was getting really battered. And for the first time in my life I hoped the Old Bill would move in and nick me. At least I'd be out of the tug-of-war nightmare.

One last surge of strength and I made the leap back on to the West Ham side. The police were moving in fast but the lads all smothered me so they couldn't see me and I crept out of the ground with my tail between my legs. As if it hadn't been a shit enough day, I decided to get a bit of revenge when we bumped into a mob of Chelsea boys later and I steamed in fists flying. I was wrestling with a big Chelsea fan when a great big, lanky West Ham lad charged in and tried to boot him with his Dr Martens. He missed and kicked me right on the nose. It busted my nose, it hurt like fuck and there was blood everywhere. I thought, It's not my day. Time to go home.

I walked through my front door, my missus looked at the black eyes, broken nose and bruises and said, 'Nice day at the football?'

Gradually, I became more and more fearless, testing myself at every match, seeing what I could get away with and stay in one piece. Sometimes I got a kick in the bollocks, sometimes I got a good hiding but all the time I was getting battle-hardened and loving it. You've got to be able to take a good hiding as well as dish it out. I've had my nose rearranged and I've been kicked in the face by Arsenal and Chelsea fans, stabbed in the back by Millwall fans, but all I wanted to do was get back into the fray the next week, and get my revenge. It was ten years of sheer madness.

I knew football and football violence had consumed my life. I told my wife, Karen, before our wedding, 'I'm sorry, but soccer comes first.' I was totally obsessed. I couldn't even be in the same room as a rival supporter. If I was doing the door at a club and opposition supporters turned up, we'd have to do them. I hated everybody except West Ham fans. It was like a primeval hatred in me. Tribal instincts running riot.

I'd had a fucking great West Ham tattoo done on my arm at Ringo's in Woolwich when I was living at Mum and Dad's. I was scared to let my mum see it and always wore long-sleeved shirts. Then, one night, I came home pissed and fell on the floor. They got me undressed to put me to bed and she saw it. She went ballistic. But I didn't care. West Ham was my life. This was my badge.

The more the authorities tried to stop us getting to games, the more ingenious ways we found to beat them. The simplest was our motors. We had a small fleet of cars between us – big Granadas, Mark 1 Lotus Cortinas, that sort of thing, so we could load them with our firm and get anywhere we wanted. We'd pull out the back seats before we left and shove a load of pool cues and chair legs underneath ready for use at the other end. We'd screw the seats back down again so if the Old Bill stopped us they wouldn't find anything that could be called an offensive weapon. We'd pull in at a service station near the ground and get tooled up. Sometimes, you'd get rival supporters' coaches in there as well. So it would all kick off in the filling station, a nightmare if you happened to be innocently pulling in for a couple of gallons of four star.

It was amazing what weapons we could produce even when we'd been searched. The *Sun* newspaper, rolled up and folded the right way, makes a vicious little cosh. One of us had ammonia in a fountain pen which was very nasty when it was squirted in the eyes. Nobody knew what had done the damage and the pen was back in the pocket looking as innocent as a ballpoint biro.

Hooliganism was spiralling out of control. It was getting really nasty, really spiteful. Soccer fans were loathed the world over. England's fans were seen as the shame of the nation. Politicians started calling for tougher penalties to wipe out the menace. But no one could understand the obsession, except the hooligans themselves. I missed only about six games in ten years. I wouldn't even go on holiday in case I missed a West Ham game. It ruled my life. I'd become addicted to violence.

I remember one weekend we borrowed a van belonging to a pop group, for whom a mate of mine was a roadie, and drove up to a Sunderland game. We left on a Friday night, with a mattress in the back to sleep on, and drove to Coventry. There were about 20 of us packed in there and we all steamed into a local nightclub and got pissed up. It kicked off inside and we had a right decent punch-up. Then we drove on to Sunderland through the night and got there at about 6.00am, most of us sleeping in the back. We stopped at a service station for breakfast then moved on to a pub. We came back and found the van smashed up. Trouble beckoned. We had a ruck at the game after the police hadn't bothered to put any officers the other side of the gates and we could run anywhere. Some of us up the front of the attack wore opposition scarves to fool the security and get among the enemy, something we'd done successfully at Chelsea matches.

Afterwards, we stopped off at Doncaster on the way back and four coaches of Newcastle fans stopped. We were in the pub 20-handed and we heard, 'You Cockney bastards,' and all of a sudden all the windows came through, there were bricks and glass everywhere and the owner was trying to stop people getting in. The Geordies had just happened to stop off for a beer on their way back from another game and we'd got another war. We went outside and headed for the van. We could hear the Geordies shouting, 'Where are the Cockney cunts? Lets get 'em.'

Me and my pal were in the back of our battered van with just a penknife to defend ourselves and I said, 'Fucking hell, we're going to get caught out here.' Then the rest of the West Ham boys appeared like the cavalry and we'd got another ruck going. Another crazy weekend for the ICF.

We'd left on the Friday and got back on the Sunday still in the same clothes, black eyes, cuts and bruises. But you just got yourself scrubbed up, a change of gear and got ready for the next round. I even sold my record collection, my clothes, anything I had to get the money together to get to the next game. I cut household spending to a minimum, went on cheap holidays to save for my football money. It cost me every penny week after week. It was total addiction. Crazy really, because there was no financial return on anything we did.

I don't say that what I did was right, but West Ham flowed through my veins. I was training as a marine engineer at the Royal Albert docks at the start of the soccer madness. I needed more than that. My reputation on the terraces gave me street cred, it gave me a name that people knew, which turned out to be invaluable in the lifestyle I finally chose, the muscle game. I was known as someone who could handle himself, a hard man, a leader. I wasn't just recognised on my home patch, I got recognised in other areas. 'Oh, that's Carlton Leach, a man you can respect.' It opened doors for me time and time again as I moved into clubland and then, inevitably, into gangland.

I know now that I was behaving totally irresponsibly with my West Ham infatuation. I was married, had a wife, a mortgage and yet was still out there getting nicked, charged with threatening behaviour, causing an affray and GBH and under observation from the football intelligence unit. I was even up in court three days before my wedding day. I was in line for some serious porridge. Even away from the terraces, the West Ham legacy was causing problems.

I was on duty one night at the Penthouse club when my footballer mate Dave Martin came in. He played professionally for Millwall but I never held that against him because he was a good bloke. I'd go to watch him sometimes, but only at away games. It would have been suicide to go to Millwall's ground in Coldblow Lane. Too many people knew me. Anyway, because he was a mate, he used to take me there on non-match days for some physiotherapy to a knee injury I'd got playing football myself. The staff took one look at my tattoo and said, 'West Ham? What the fuck are you doing here?'

Dave said, 'It's OK, he's with me.' We had a bit of a laugh about it.

When he came that night to the Penthouse, some Millwall fans were there and asked him who he was with. He said, 'Carlton Leach, ICF West Ham.' They looked horrified but we never gave it another thought. Dave's girlfriend was the best mate of my first wife's, so it was just a social thing and he was quite entitled to be seen with me. But the next time he walked on to the pitch, he got a torrent of abuse. 'You fucking West Ham supporter. You wanker. You scumbag, Martin.' They made his life a misery. So it wasn't surprising that he soon got a transfer to Wimbledon. I went to watch him play there, neutral territory, but still got into bother as we were drinking in the players' bar. Some Crystal Palace supporters were there and started slagging off West Ham. I kept my tongue for Dave's sake. But then I couldn't take it any more. They were rubbishing my beloved West Ham and I had to fight them. A big ruck kicked off and Dave Bassett, the Wimbledon manager, was right in the middle tying to calm everything down. That was the strength of my feelings. I couldn't even be in normal civilised company without jumping to the defence of West Ham with my fists.

I revelled in the fear we brought to towns and cities all over the country, the way they shut the pubs and shops when they knew the ICF was in town, the way a path would clear through 10,000 fans as the 300-strong West Ham mob swaggered through the streets, standing our ground in the face of bombardments from snooker balls, bricks and chair legs, defying the police as they charged in with horses and batons, dragging you off and giving you a good hiding. I loved it.

I had gained such notoriety by now that Thames TV did a documentary about soccer hooliganism which featured me and several other members of the ICF. I play it occasionally and wince at the bantam cocks pictured on film bragging about the violence. Then it was a £50 fine if you got nicked. Now you're talking six months for just swearing at a game. The spies from the football intelligence unit were everywhere and things had to change. I still go to the odd West Ham game, but that urge to run amok and scare the shit out of people has long gone. I've got different priorities now.

Self-preservation also played a big part in me quitting the terraces. It was only a matter of time before I got nicked for something serious. I got a tip-off from a copper I knew that Scotland Yard was launching a fucking great anti-hooligan operation. He'd seen an ops room board containing dozens of suspects. And whose photo was at the top? Yours truly.

He said, 'Do yourself a favour, Carlton; knock it on the head or you are going to get nicked for something heavy.' I think he was talking about charges for conspiracy to cause violence or something like that with a probable five-year stretch. The geezer did me a big favour. At first, you think, Oh bollocks, they won't stop us. A lot of the other lads down the Britannia thought the same way and we said we'd carry on as normal. Then, one night, I was walking home and I thought, What the fuck am I doing? I've been going ten years as one of the top soccer thugs, I've had a good run, now it's time to stop.

I took it easy for a while but then I split up with my wife and the lure of the terraces drew me back. I was living in a flat with three other geezers who were all hard-case soccer thugs. We were out in pubs drinking, shoulder to shoulder with undercover cops from the football unit. Our flat was all decked out in West Ham gear, we had knives, coshes and all sorts of tools round the place. It was like battle HQ for the ICF and I was up to my ears again even though I knew I was being targeted. But I knew that my time was running out. So I told my mates one day, 'Oh sod it, I'm going back home.'

Another mate had just split up with his missus so he took over my room. Just a matter of days later the police stormed in mob-handed in a big Scotland Yard clean-up operation. They thought he was me, steamed into his bedroom and turned the place over. It should have been me, a lucky escape but another warning.

Because I'd not been to many matches after the copper's warning, I'd missed being caught on the surveillance cameras at the West Ham games so when the police questioned me they hadn't got anything on me. But I knew it was time to back off. I'd had some great times, done some mad things, but I had to shut the door on all that now. No more trying to be the hardest of the soccer hard men, no more travelling hundreds of miles to challenge the other firms for the dubious title of Britain's most feared superthug. I couldn't really explain what it was all about, why we had this need for violence. But I remember well the TV producer who made the *Hooligans* programme saying on an afternoon talk show, 'If there was a war, these boys would be winning medals.' I think he was right. It's no good sending a computer wizard or a stockbroker to fight a war. If you've got 500 troops in action, you've got to have natural, born leaders, people who can inspire that extra bit of courage in the face of danger. Someone's got to get up and lead the charge. That was me in the soccer world. I knew I was a natural leader, and because I was also a good talker, I could get people to follow me. Even though my arse was pouting, I'd go in first. 'Come on, you cunts, we can do this lot,' and I knew they would be right behind me. I was a general on the terraces with troops who would probably have been a credit to the nation on a battlefield, but because our arena was football, because we were seen to be wrecking the nation's favourite sport, we were deemed to be the lowest of the low. But those same boys will go and win you wars. And if the world suffered a major catastrophe and we were left without power, food, all the basic commodities we take for granted, who would you depend on then? Who would be the survivors and providers? Who would know how to go out with a fucking great Bowie knife, catch an animal, skin and cook it over an open fire? I'd be out there doing that and so would most of the people who were condemned as brainless morons for soccer violence. Ninety per cent of the population would be fucked if they couldn't pop out to Sainsbury's or Tesco's.

Life is about survival and football taught me about survival. I learned about sticking together, trusting each other, inspiring people to beat the odds. It's all double standards in polite society. Put two boxers in the ring and people will pay £100 a ticket to watch them knock fuck out of each other, even to the point of a coma, but if I walk up to another football fan who is wearing a different scarf and punch him in the face, I am a dangerous hooligan who should be locked up.

My passion for West Ham as a football team never totally waned. My whole mood for a week could be determined by the West Ham result. If I watched them on Sky TV getting beaten by one of the teams I hated, I wouldn't talk for a day. If anyone spoke to me, I could as easily thump them as give a reply.

One of the funniest things about the hooligan days was the collection of regional accents I built up. As part of our cover we practised Scouse, Brummie, Geordie, all sorts of accents to help us penetrate the opposition. I can still do a passable 'Haway the lads' that fooled a good few Newcastle fans. Not exactly Rory Bremner, but not bad when you consider my normal accent is about as Cockney as Alf Garnett.

There were a lot of laughs among the kickings, the brickbats, the bottles and the knifings. We were coming back to London by train one night from a Newcastle game and we'd had a drink and decided to break into the buffet car. The alarm went off but the driver didn't want to stop with a bunch of hooligans on board so he carried on towards King's Cross. By now a fucking great food fight had broken out. There were bits of chicken, sandwiches, crisps, nuts, all sorts of grub being lobbed about and the lads had got stuck into the bar sloshing down beers and spirits. But our lot were in a really good mood. So they were going through the carriages handing out snacks and drinks free to everyone on board. There were old-age pensioners, Australians, some business types and they hadn't a clue what was happening. The boys were going down the train like waiters asking, 'What would you like, luv? Nice gin and tonic or a nice port and lemon?' Then they found some half-bottles of champagne and popped them open and were giving bubbly to everybody. Then came the cigars and cigarettes. We were lighting them up for the old boys and pouring them large brandies. By the end of the journey, we had half of them pissed. The old dears were saying, 'Oh, aren't they lovely boys? Their mums must be proud.'

As we approached King's Cross, the Old Bill were gathering. We were saying to each other, 'Don't walk off with anything, leave it on the train.' We'd had a good drink and a good feast so we didn't want any more. But a couple of other passengers couldn't resist filling up their bags with the nicked goodies, and – Wallop! – the Old Bill was on them and they were done for theft. Nothing to do with West Ham. We walked past shouting 'Wankers', having a right laugh. The police weren't at all amused when they walked into the buffet car and found it littered end to end with food and bottles and realised that all they'd nicked were a couple of pissed pensioners on their way home from a day trip to Doncaster.

7

Dutch Courage

The nagging doubt in the back of my mind transformed swiftly into real anxiety as the big Mercedes turned on to the darkened forest roads just off the motorway. Was this a hit? Had we been set up? Phil and me were on a minding job in Amsterdam and this was foreign territory to us, well off our usual Essex manor.

We'd taken a huge wodge of cash – I reckon about £250,000 – to Holland for some underworld pals to pay off a debt. Seemed simple enough. Probably drugs cash, but we didn't really want to know too much. All we had to do was deliver it safely and collect our fee. A minding job, my speciality.

Now we sensed real danger. The trees seemed to close in on us as the headlights cut through the night, picking out huge dark pines, then the shape of a startled deer. The Dutch driver slowed down and stopped. We were on a road that was little more than a dirt track. He chatted briefly to his pal in the passenger seat and then reversed into a small gap beside the road.

Me and Phil tensed up. We looked at each other uneasily. We were in a dangerous game and knew it. But now we were getting seriously spooked. I whispered, 'I think they're going to top us.'

What do we do? Should we grab the Dutch guys in a headlock and strangle them from behind before they pulled their shooters on us? We knew they were tooled up. They were suited and booted in good quality gear but the bulges under their jackets were unmistakable. They were like us, professionals in the minding game, class bodyguards for a powerful Dutch mob dealing drugs big time.

'Shall we take 'em now?' I said to Phil under my breath, hoping they wouldn't understand my Cockney English. I talk fast anyway so there was a chance they wouldn't know what we were going to to do. I tensed up ready for action. I was ready to throw 16-and-a-half stone of muscle at the driver and sod the consequences. If the car roared off and hit a tree, fuck it, we'd take our chances.

Then, suddenly, there was another brief conversation between the Dutch boys. One of them laughed and the silver Merc swept off again. The tension eased a bit but we were still jittery. Were they searching for somewhere even quieter to top us? Our driver was clearly looking for another road somewhere in the woods, slowing and peering intently through the windscreen. But what for?

All sorts of things were still rushing through my mind, most of them bad. We still couldn't be sure the danger was over. Hopefully, we weren't going to have to fight our way out of this one after all. But the fact of the matter was that we were caught up in a big-time drugs deal and were snaking our way through a forest in Holland in the back of a gangland limo with two geezers with guns calling the tune in a language we didn't understand. I didn't like it. Neither did Phil. OK, we were in a high-risk business, but I wasn't about to become a casualty. I'd seen too many mates end up on a mortuary slab to take any chances.

By now we were both like coiled springs in the back seat. One wrong move and we'd have a madhouse in the motor. Then the tall trees of the forest gave way to houses with nice gardens and tidy hedges. We were obviously in a decent sort of suburb somewhere south of Amsterdam and you could feel the relief as the driver started peering out of his window obviously looking for a particular property. He nudged his pal and they chuckled among themselves. We hadn't a clue what was going on, not a fucking inkling. And in my wildest dreams I could never have imagined what was going to happen in the next 24 hours.

Now the Merc was slowing again. We'd found our destination. The driver pulled into the driveway of a beautiful house, more like a millionaire's mansion, set among immaculate lawns and shrubs, and parked the car on the gravel beside a Porsche and two BMWs.

'Come now,' said one of the Dutch geezers. 'Come inside.'

Then a smiling woman in her forties came to the door and

beckoned us forward. Our two English mates, who'd been following in a sleek, blue BMW driven by another couple of Dutch blokes, drew up behind us.

Well, I'd never seen anything like it. The house turned out to be Amsterdam's premier knocking shop. The classiest whore house in town, girls at £150 an hour. Shagarama. And we'd been given the freedom of the city. That's right, said our Dutch hosts, you can have any girl you like, or as many girls as you like for as long as you like, and the treat's on us.

I was boggle-eyed. There must have been about 14 or 15 girls working there, every one looking like a fucking film star. There was a heated indoor swimming pool, a Jacuzzi, there was puff and there was coke and there was every kind of booze.

The main man of the Dutch gangsters cleared the brothel of all the other punters. It was unbelievable. There was a comfortable bar with soft seats and cosy lighting, a piano bar, lovely bedrooms, it was fantastic. For a boy from the back streets of East Ham this was fucking bliss, literally. This, it turned out, was our 'thank you' bonus for the successful transfer of the cash that we'd minded from the UK to Holland. Everyone was happy. Now it was our turn to get very, very happy indeed. Far from wanting to blow us away with a .45 as we had feared just a couple of hours earlier, they were now intent on trying to kill us with a serious overdose of sexual activity.

We'd lived with the danger for days, transporting the cash from Essex, through Dover and across France and Belgium to Holland, and we'd got through the panic of a possible hit in the forest and now we were ready to party. It was the first time I'd been asked to do a foreign minding job. I'd been in muscle most of my life, from football hooliganism and nightclub bouncer to registered and respected security adviser. Never been averse to a bit of violence, never been afraid of anyone in my life.

This Amsterdam trip was different, off my home patch, not understanding the language, not knowing what was going on half the time, I was hyped up to the hilt and ready to blow.

I'd realised we were involved with the big boys half-way through the journey. We'd stopped at a petrol station in Belgium to fill up the Ford Granada and I saw bundles of notes slipping out from under the back seat where they'd been hidden. I didn't count the cash but I knew it was a big lump. Me and Phil wouldn't have been hired for the job if it was a piddling little amount. Nothing much was said about it. 'It's to settle a bill,' we were told.

Yeah, we knew what big lumps of money and Amsterdam meant. So we didn't ask questions. We were there to make sure it got delivered safely. There was a lot of ripping off of drugs money going on, villains against villains. Me and Phil had got big reputations in the muscle game and the blokes who had hired us knew we wouldn't get stuffed by anyone.

We sailed through English and French Customs and border checks no problem, me and Phil in the back, the blokes who'd hired us in the front; we didn't even get a second glance, let alone a tug, and drove to a hotel in downtown Amsterdam, unchallenged at any point, to meet up with the Dutch connections. We booked into our hotel, had a shower, got changed and prepared to go out on the town for a bit of R and R. We met up with the Dutch boys that evening in a downstairs coffee bar just off the reception area and the money was handed over.

Like I say, it was a lot of bucks. I don't know whether it was a complete payment or a part payment, but everybody seemed very happy with things. Our people and the foreign boys were all sitting round a table chatting and laughing. Then there were another two fellas standing watching, not having a drink, not saying anything, obviously the Dutch gang's minders just as we were the English fellas' minders. The brawn minding the brains. Then there were a couple of other geezers who were either Spanish or Italian. It was all buzzing with about three or four different languages being spoken, deals being done, a lot of happy back-slapping. This was professional villainy going on and I was in the thick of it and, I must say, at that moment in time, loving every minute of it.

Then the silver Merc, and a 7-series BMW arrived. 'These are for you,' said one of our hosts, 'we are all going out for the night.'

Lovely stuff, I thought. This is the business. I've cracked it.

I didn't show too much interest in what was going on. That wasn't my job. I was there to get the money delivered and my people back in one piece. So, job almost done, I was ready to rumble in Amsterdam. Me and Phil were ushered into the back of the Merc and the two Dutch bodyguards got in the front. The two other English geezers we were with got in the BMW and we all set off in a two-car convoy. It was only when we were up and rolling that we suddenly felt vulnerable. Perhaps it had all gone too easy and now we had to pay the price. Getting topped was not in the job description but we knew it was always a possibility when big money was involved. We weren't carrying any weapons because we were on foreign territory. But we knew for sure the Dutch team were tooled up. We had survived the scare in the pine forest by the skin of our teeth and now here we were sitting in a brothel with a bunch of beautiful, half-naked girls getting stoned out of our brains. I said to Phil, 'Fuck me, another few seconds in that Merc and we might have blown the whole fucking thing apart. If we'd grabbed the bodyguards like we said, we'd have crashed the car, probably been badly hurt and would have ended up as real targets at the top of the Dutch mobs' hit list and probably started an international gang war. We've had a lucky escape, mate.'

Lucky? We didn't know what luck was for the next night and day. We were invited to have any of the girls, or as many as we wanted at any one time, to do anything we wanted. We stripped off naked and slid into the pool with the bevy of beauties. My eyes were on stalks. I'd always been a bit of a shagger, never could keep my dick in my trousers, but I'd never seen anything like this before. The Dutch bodyguards sat at a table and laid out some drug samples for us to try, good quality cannabis, a bit of cocaine, whatever we wanted to get us fuelled up. Not that we needed anything to stoke us up but we had a dabble. It seemed rude not to. The main man sloshed up some champagne and then we were in the pool again swimming about, trying to look cool, like we hadn't really been ready to rip the heads off two Dutch blokes an hour or two earlier.

Now all four of us English visitors were getting the VIP treatment in a luxury pool with 14 dishy girls, stark naked, and not really knowing quite what we should do. I didn't know it but, apparently, the girls weren't allowed to make any advances to us so we were swimming up and down like it's Bethnal Green fucking public baths, ogling the tits and not doing much else. I said to my mate, 'What do we do now?'

He went, 'I dunno, Carlton.'

One of the Dutch blokes saw our quandary, came over and told us that if we fancied any of the girls we had to approach them. 'You've got all 14 for yourselves all night,' he said, 'have a good time.'

Now we'd got the green light. I'd had my eye on a nice dark-haired girl with a fantastic figure. She gave me a really nice smile, which caught my eye, and I swam over to her, all rippling muscles and a smile like the Cheshire Cat, and got straight into a close body embrace. Her name was Anneka if I remember rightly. We soon got out of the pool and went to a sort of sauna room and bedroom at the back and were straight into a passionate clinch. But I'd had a lot to drink and a bit of gear and I couldn't get a hard on. Fourteen birds and I couldn't raise it. I was gutted. But Anneka wasn't having any of that. She went down on me, she massaged me, she masturbated herself to excite me, she went to town for about an hour 'til she got me up and running. That did it. Afterwards, I couldn't wait to get back into the pool for afters. This was the night of a lifetime, fantasy island, and I wanted to make the most of it.

Then three of the girls standing in the corner in the shallow end caught my eye. Two of them were playing with each other while the third one watched. All three were gorgeous. I couldn't believe my eyes. I got out of the pool and walked round to them.

'You want these?' asked one of our hosts.

'These two, yeah,' I said.

'No, take three, take four,' he insisted.

'You must be bleeding joking,' I said.

'No, you are going nowhere else, you take all four and fuck them,' he laughed.

'No, bollocks,' I said, 'I don't know how I'm going to manage with two, let alone four.'

So it was off to the king-sized bed with another pair of game-for-anything dollybirds. It was blowing my mind.

It wasn't like a normal brass house. There were waitresses bringing drinks, as much food as you wanted, big baths to keep yourself clean in, a free and easy atmosphere, a real top-notch advert for legalised prostitution. And I was taking full advantage. The two girls gave me a top-to-toe massage with beautiful smelling oils. Then they had sex with each other in front of me. One was a tall blonde and one was a tomboyish little readhead. They'd done that before, that's for sure. I was steaming again.

In the middle of all this stumbled Phil with a girl, which turned out to be the one I'd shagged earlier, Anneka.

'Mind if I come in?' he asked, which was a bit silly as he

was already in the room and we were all at it and not giving a shit about anything. So he walked across the room and started to run a hot bath. I was on the bed giving it all that, one girl in front, one behind ... 'Oooh, baby ... oooh, lovely,' putting on a bit of a show. Phil was in this massive corner bath with Anneka, rubbing her tits with foam, but the longer he stayed in the water the limper his tackle got.

'Let's have the bed, mate,' he said. 'Yeah, no problem, Phil ...'

We swapped over, I got in the bath with my two and Phil got on the bed with his bird. Mine were playing with each other again and I got them to gee up Phil ... 'Come on, baby, fucky fucky ...' But because he'd had too much booze he couldn't get it up. He was furious. Finally, he jumped off the bed in frustration and he's stuck his big toe straight into the used Durex I'd thrown on the floor earlier. He took one look, lifted his foot in the air and shouted, 'You dirty bastard ... This could only happen to me ... of all the people ... I end up with your fucking dirty used johnny on the end of my toe.'

We all had a bit of a laugh then got back down to it in a right old orgy, all five of us in the same room. What a night. We were still there at 8.30 the next morning.

Our beautiful hostess sent us on our way with a slap-up breakfast and a bundle of memories I'll never forget. Me and Phil laughed about it all that day back at our hotel. In my everyday world of fear and violence it was one of the great highs.

Sordid, maybe, but then my life back home could be

equally as sordid as I found myself getting trapped in a vicious circle of drug-taking, booze and violence. Me and my pals were running amok. The Essex Boys were out of control. And it was all destined to end in tragedy for Tony, Pat and Craig in that snow-swept country lane in Essex. Amsterdam was a happy blip on a clock ticking relentlessly towards disaster.

8

Sorted

No one, but no one, messes with my family. And when I discovered that my dad was being seriously pissed around over a car, I moved into action like fucking Superman.

I'd got the motor from Tony Tucker, a top-of-the-range, leather-upholstered Granada Scorpio and drove it over to East Ham. My dad had never had a nice car so I thought this was a chance to say, 'There you go. Thanks for everything.' His face was a picture when he saw it. At last, a decent set of wheels to get him and Mum about. But first it needed a bit of work on it, a respray and a few mechanical repairs, though it was basically a good motor. Dad had just retired, so he and Mum would have plenty of spare time now to get out and about a bit, visit a few relatives, go down to Southend in the summer. It would be lovely.

I'd been looking after a bloke who'd got a car repair garage and stables on a farm in Essex and he owed me a favour. Several favours in fact. I'd lent him money which he hadn't paid back; Dad had also lent him money up front, and he hadn't got that back either. He had generally fucked us around for a couple of years. I reckoned a nice respray job on the Scorpio and a mechanical overhaul would help settle the score.

I took the Scorpio in and couldn't wait for the day I picked it up, hopefully now looking in showroom condition. We waited and we waited, days then weeks. I saw other cars going in, getting done and moving on. But nothing happened with Dad's motor. I was never a patient man at the best of times. Now I was getting angry. I told him, 'If this car isn't done the next time I come down I'm going to get a baseball bat and smash every other car in here.'

I thought it had worked when I got a call a couple of days later saying Dad could pick it up. But as soon as he started driving it home, the front bumper fell off, the panelwork was shaking, and instruments weren't working properly. It was a right old bodge. Now I love my dad and anyone who takes the piss is asking for real trouble. I said, 'Dad, give me the car. I'm going to sort this.'

I went to the yard and parked outside. The bloke wasn't there. His workmates said he was down the pub. By now I was fuming. I got myself a gun, got in the car and went looking for him. I'd taken it personally because Dad was so disappointed and I was seething. I thought, I'm going to kill this cunt.

This happened while I was still pumping steroids into my veins and, because of my addiction, I was getting things all out of proportion in my head and all I could think about was how the bastard had abused my friendship when I'd helped him out, and how he'd insulted my dad by handing him over a duff motor. It was irrational behaviour but that's how I was at the time.

I couldn't find him anywhere and sat and waited at the yard until he turned up. I wasn't getting any happier. When he finally arrived, I said, 'What's happened with the car?'

He didn't know I was tooled up. He laughed nervously and said, 'Oh, that will be in next.'

I said, 'Come here, cunt, I want a talk with you,' and marched him into the tack room beside the stables. I said, 'You're taking the piss, ain'tcha?'

He half-laughed. He knew this was no joke. Then I pulled out the gun. His jaw dropped and there was a look of sheer terror in his eyes. 'You mess with me and I'll fucking kill you now,' I said. But again he laughed. I let off a shot which whacked into the ceiling sending debris down on one of the saddles hanging in there. I shoved him down on the floor and pistol-whipped him with the gun. He wasn't laughing now. Blood was trickling down his face and he was shitting himself. He was down on his hands and knees on the tack room floor. I got the gun and shoved it in his mouth. 'Don't you ever fuck with me or my family or you're a dead man,' I yelled. 'You think I'm some sort of mug?'

By now he was screaming. I took the gun out of his mouth intending to put a shot into his leg, hurting him, warning him, but not killing him. He knocked the gun aside in sheer panic as I fired and another bullet went into the wall.

He started wailing, 'It's not my fault, it's those cunts in there.'

I was steaming by now. 'So you're a fucking grass as well, are you?' I said. 'You're telling me it's the others, nothing to do with you. We'll see about that.'

I went storming back into the garage and let off a volley of shots into a van they'd just finished spraying. They'd done a lovely job. The sort of job they should have done on my dad's car. One of the lumps working there came out holding the bumper of Dad's car.

'He says it's you that's fucked up the job,' I said.

'No way, no, no,' he said in a panic.

I let off more shots – Bang! Bang! – one each side of him. He stood there paralysed with fear. Then a little mechanic walked in to see what the fuck was happening. He took one look at the shooter, then the bullet holes and the shot-up van and pissed himself on the spot.

'Did you fuck up as well?' I said.

He was too scared to answer. It was all getting out of control. I was walking up and down with the gun in my hand. Fortunately, a mate of mine arrived.

'Carlton, calm down, calm down. It's not worth getting a life sentence for.' He persuaded me to put the shooter away before someone got killed.

The next thing I knew, the boss man was on the phone to a Ford parts supplier ordering new this and new that for the Scorpio. His hands were shaking so much he could hardly hold the phone. It was time to back off.

Within a couple of days, I got a call saying the car was done, repaired, resprayed and ready to roll. It was a fucking picture. Immaculate. The old man was the proudest owner in the street. I said to the geezer who had caused the problems, 'Why? Why did it have to come to that? Why did you need to take the piss?' He didn't have an answer. He was still shaken by my onslaught in the workshop.

Then he looked at me straight in the eye and said, 'Were you really going to shoot me?'

I said, 'Yes, I fucking was. I thought you were mugging me off and I was going to give you one through the leg to teach you a fucking lesson.'

He knew I wasn't kidding.

Months later, rough justice worked in his favour. He was having bother with a team of fellas who were claiming a piece of his land and had turned up in a JCB to take it by force. They were plotted up on the disputed site in a Range Rover, a car and a van waiting for the digger to arrive. We roused two other geezers to come along and went to the site armed with baseball bats and knuckledusters ready to defend the position. The main man laying claim to the land was sitting in a new Jag at one of the two entrances. Battle positions were drawn.

Me, my mate and the two others were all training, all in the muscle business, all on steroids and we must have looked a fearsome quartet. We marched up to the Jag where three of the other side were sitting.

'You come to take my mate's land?' I said.

Without waiting for a reply, I swung my baseball bat and took out the windscreen. Big Mark, 6ft 4in and 20 stone, walked to the back window and punched a fucking great hole in it. Lucky for him he was wearing a knuckleduster. Not so lucky for the Jag and its cowering occupants. The geezers couldn't believe it.

'Hold on, hold on,' one of them shouted. No way. I was cooking on gas now. I walked up to their brand-new Range Rover and started a demolition job on the windows. Whack! Whack! Glass was flying everywhere. Bang! I started on the lights, anything I could smash. The ground was littered with broken glass like the aftermath of a motorway pile-up. I gave the Range Rover serious grief end to end, bumper to bumper. Then one of them tried to get away in the van. I was after it like Linford Christie and beat the shit out of the back window. Three nil to us.

Not surprisingly, the claim on the land was withdrawn the next day. A phonecall to my mate and it was all settled amicably, like our own personal dispute, sorted gangland style. A few months earlier, I'd had a gun in his mouth threatening to blow him away. Now we'd stood shoulder to shoulder to defend his property. He kept the land. We restored a friendship. Doing nothing was never an option. We weren't into expensive court cases, clever talk from lawyers and months of litigation. In those days, once I'd pressed the go button, or someone had pressed it for me, it was all action, no turning back 'til the job was done.

★   ★   ★

Another car job turned out to be just about the most enjoyable take-away of the year. A smart-arsed Nigerian car dealer had rumped a good pal of mine for over £25,000. So we took away the entire stock of motors from his forecourt to even the score and pay off the debt.

Kim Webber is one of those diamond geezers in the murky old world of muscle. Generous, shrewd, funny, but hard as nails when necessary. As I was desperately shaking off the steroid habit and all its problems, plus the devastating shock of the Rettendon murders, I moved down to Southend to try to sort my head out. Kim, whom I'd first met at Basildon Hospital after Pat Tate had been shot, took me under his wing, so to speak. He put a few bits of work my way and helped me through many black days with his wit and generosity. Kim did a bit of debt collection, a bit of car dealing, and got me a few security jobs. He was well respected and well liked as a geezer who stood his corner in a bar and could have you splitting your sides with his zany humour. He became a true friend at a time when I really needed a friend. And when he told me he had been ripped off for 25 grand, I was more than ready to repay a favour.

Kim told me over a drink at King's Club, Canvey Island, that the Nigerian guy in Manor Park owed him the money for a bit of business they'd done a year earlier but was refusing to pay up. I said right away I'd pull up a team, head for East London and sort it for him. Manor Park, after all, was my old patch and I still knew plenty of faces there.

Kim was reluctant to start with. 'No, no, don't get involved, Carlton,' he said. Perhaps he thought I was still unable to control my emotions and we'd have a war on our hands. But those days were over, hopefully, and I was seeing straight again.

I could see Kim had got a problem but I wasn't going to push it unless he said so. He was trying to sort it out himself, so I stood down for a couple of weeks. I knew if it involved Nigerians, it might be tricky. In the international league of crime, the Nigerians are right up there in the top ten, masters of fraud with some of the most sophisticated scams in criminal history to their credit. A lot of them are so fucking bent they couldn't sleep straight in their beds if they were nailed down. Our current problem wasn't exactly super league but it involved a friend and it needed sorting. So I was pleased when Kim came to me a couple of weeks later and said, 'Let's do it, let's get my money.'

We drove up to Manor Park and tried to settle it peacefully. Kim played the good guy, talking nicely to the Nigerian, I hovered about on the forecourt among the cars for sale looking sinister but saying nothing. I could see the Nigerian was getting more and more cocky because we weren't doing anything heavy. I joined in.

'You owe my friend the money, you've got to pay it. Let's come to some sort of arrangement.'

Nobody could say we weren't giving him a fair chance. With that, he decided to play the race card. 'You're only doing this because I'm black,' he ranted. 'You wouldn't be giving me hassle if I was a white boy.'

That really needled me. Racist is one thing I'm not, as readers will know by now. I was on a patch where I'd grown up with black kids from childhood and they were still my friends.

I looked straight in his eyes and said, 'I know a fucking

sight more black people round here than you do. And I've been best man at the wedding of two black friends. So don't give me all that shit.'

With that, we decided to quit talking and start some action. We said if he didn't cough up £2,000 immediately for starters, we'd have no choice but to take one of his motors in lieu of payment. And if he didn't find the rest of the 25 grand within two weeks, we'd be back for the rest of his motors.

'Come back tomorrow. I'll give you £2,000 then,' he said.

Not fucking likely. 'Money now or we take that Merc,' I said.

'I'll give you £2,000 a week 'til it's cleared,' he said, getting a bit desperate as he sensed we now meant business.

After 12 months of fannying about over the money, we reckoned it was highly unlikely that he'd suddenly produce it unless we applied a little pressure.

'Right,' we said, 'we'll agree to the deal. But we're taking the Merc as security.' He looked furious. Before he could argue, we grabbed the keys and jumped in the Mercedes. We rolled off the forecourt and headed for a lock-up where we plotted the motor up safely out of sight.

The next day, Kim met him again and – surprise, surprise – he produced £2,000 in twenties.

'Where's my car?' he demanded.

We both reckoned the slippery fucker had only produced the cash to buy a bit of time so we told him we were hanging on to the Merc 'til the debt was settled in full. He was livid. And the next day he was phoning Kim and threatening to get Yardie gangsters in to kill us, to get the notorious A-Team of

North London villains – otherwise known as the Adams family – down to Southend as well as all sorts of hard-case villains to sort us out.

When Kim told me, it was like a red rag to a bull. 'Right,' I said, 'I'm going to do him.' So it was into combat gear, army drills, black coat, black gloves, black SWAT cap and I was set for action. The geezer had called me on and I was ready. We'd given the bloke a break, tried to be fair and now he was showering us with a load of heavy crap and trying to scare us off. That doesn't work with me and it doesn't work with my firm.

Kim came round and saw that I was tooled up. 'No, not that,' he said. 'It's not that important.'

But, by now, it was personal. Reputations were at stake.

'OK, Kim,' I said, 'no violence, but let's do a take-away. Let's have the motors off the forecourt to cover the debt. No messing now. Let's do it.'

I got a hand-picked team together ... big Ian Wadley from *Hard Bastards*. He's black. My Sid, 6ft 5in of dreadlocked West Indian. Another Sid, of African origin. Some of my other regular heavies acted as drivers. There was no way the Nigerian geezer could say this was racist and start all that voodoo crap.

We sent Fearless in first as a moody customer just to check the place over. He went round the back and shinned up a lamp-post to get a look into some flats close by to check there weren't hordes of Nigerians waiting to jump out on us. It was all clear.

About six or seven of us were waiting at my dad's house

for a call from Fearless. When it came, we piled into two cars and headed for the garage. We kept out of sight round the corner as big Sid and one of the other fellas strolled casually in and started chatting to an Asian guy who'd been left in charge.

'All right mate? How are you doing?' they asked. Before he could answer we were in through the doors and ripping out the phones. No sign of the Nigerian. We pinned the Asian guy down in his chair.

'Where are the fucking car keys?'

He reckoned he didn't know. Dave pulled out a stun gun, leaned over and gave him a whack with it. Zzzzz!! He was fucking petrified. We told him our beef wasn't with him and if he co-operated and gave us the keys and car registration documents he wouldn't get hurt.

'I don't know, I don't know,' he whimpered. It was obviously bollocks because he'd been left in charge and couldn't sell a car without the key or paperwork. Dave changed his mind with another zap from the electric stun gun.

'They're over there, they're in the cupboard,' he squealed.

We helped ourselves to what we needed off the forecourt as two of the boys stood guard in case the opposition turned up. Kim started with a nice BMW and our driver was away in it. Then he picked a Saab turbo and a couple of others and the take-away was complete. Lovely job.

The Nigerian geezer made some rumbling noises over the next couple of weeks about what he was going to do to us, but nothing came of it. Kim held on to the motors for a couple of weeks in case he volunteered the money – fat chance of that – and then put them through a second-hand car auction and recovered his lost cash. He paid the boys a day's wages and rough justice prevailed again.

It was the first time Kim had seen me at work in true muscle mode. He said, 'I'm fucking glad I wasn't on the receiving end of that.' He knew then that I walked the walk.

★   ★   ★

On the subject of motors, I must mention one job that went very pear-shaped but gave us a good laugh in the process. My mate Mick was helping me with a bit of debt-collecting. The bloke we were after for a nice few thousand quid had a couple of tasty mates we knew might give trouble. Mick, a nice laid-back fella with a bit of form, but sound as a pound in a crisis, said he'd pick me up because my motor was in for a service.

We set off towards the geezer's home in Wickford but, before we got there, we saw his vehicle outside a farm shop and him and his mates buying some vegetables. Mick pulled the car in behind them.

'Right,' I said 'I'll get some tools from the boot and we'll tackle them here.'

'OK,' said Mick.

I dashed round the back of the car and opened the boot. Fuck me. It was full of Barbie dolls, My Little Pony, roller blades, all sorts of kids stuff. Not a tool in sight. Then Mick remembered he'd picked up his girlfriend's Toyota Corolla instead of his own car that morning and it was packed with her little girls' stuff. I looked at Mick, he looked at me and we looked at the tasty geezers we were supposed to take on.

'I hope this fucking Barbie is loaded,' I said, picking up one of the dolls. With that, we both creased up laughing, jumped in the car and giggled all the way home. Another day would do for this one.

9

Viva España

The women and children were packing their bags and leaving. The Essex Boys had hit town and were on a rampage that sent shudders through the holiday island. A four-day binge in the clubs and bars of Tenerife had seen us running out of control and frightening the life out of decent, honest holidaymakers, ending up with me so pissed I ran stark-bollock-naked along the seafront in full view of everybody. We hadn't meant to scare anyone, but the sight of 18 to 20 hard-cases shoving drink down their necks like there was no tomorrow had sent out enough warning signals for people in our hotel to start booking out early to avoid any trouble. I can't blame them, but trouble was on the agenda from the moment we flew in. We were partying and we wanted everyone else to be enjoying themselves as well.

Unfortunately, it doesn't work that way. We were giving off the sort of dangerous vibes that made sane people want to be somewhere else very rapidly, which was a pity because we really hadn't wanted to ruin anyone else's hard-earned break in the sun.

We'd descended on Tenerife mob-handed when I heard that a pal of mine who owned Bobby's Bar, a favourite watering hole of ours in the days when I visited the island with Nigel Benn and Tony Tucker, was in trouble over claims that he'd tried it on with another bloke's girlfriend. I didn't believe it from the start. Joe wasn't that sort of fella. Nevertheless, Phil, who knew the girl at the centre of it all, was adamant that we should get up a team and fly out there to sort it out one way or the other. For Joe's sake I agreed. I reckoned that if he didn't have someone acting as a sort of referee, he could come to serious harm. He was a lovely fella, popular with everyone on the island, and I didn't want to see him get carved up over a bit of nonsense like this.

I told Phil that I didn't think Joe would be silly enough to grab someone else's girlfriend and risk upsetting people who could make a lot of trouble for him. She was insisting he'd mauled her in his office at the back of the club. But the Joe I knew was a real gent and I didn't think it rang true at all. There was only one way to sort it – the firm would fly in to see justice done.

I got together some of my best boys – Ian Woodley, Dave King, Phil, Gary Grant, Dave Davis, Micky Bowman, Dal – and booked flights on the next plane out to the Canaries for a four-day stay. By then, Joe had got word of a team coming out from London and was getting worried. He phoned one of my mates and said he was going to leave Tenerife. He said he hadn't touched Phil's girlfriend and wasn't prepared to hang around to get grief for something he hadn't done. I called him up and told him to stay put. I wanted to hear his side of the story. I reassured him that nothing was going to happen to him.

We arrived in Tenerife after a fucking awful journey – six hours' delay at Gatwick – and by then we were all pissed up and lagging. That was the start of a bad four days for the island. Danny Harrison and some of the boys living out there had booked us into a good hotel. We rolled up in taxis well fired up and straight away you could sense the nervousness of the staff and guests.

We checked in quickly and then headed straight for Bobby's Bar in Playa de las Americas to sort out the matter in hand. The place was packed as we walked in mob-handed. There was a sudden hush as we asked the bar staff, 'Is Joe here?'

He appeared from his office, looking somewhere between apprehensive and shit-scared. I said, 'It's all right, Joe, we've just come to get this sorted. No one's going to get hurt.'

I told Phil and Joe to go into the office together and talk it through. I knew there had to be two sides to the story. This could be sorted between two grown-up men without the need for heavy measures. Sure enough, they came out together after ten minutes all smiles and the best of mates again. As I'd suspected, the girl had given Phil a complete load of fanny. Rather than Joe trying it on with her, she had tried to get Joe into bed then got all bitchy when he turned her down. Relief all round. Business out of the way in record time. But now we'd got four days to kill ... and we were in party mood.

We were hitting the vodkas, Jack Daniel's and Pina Coladas in Bobby's Bar when a firm we knew from Billericay came in — Jason Draper, Joe Wright, his old man, and about eight other tasty lumps. They were partying, too. So now we were about 18-handed and on a roll. Well, Bobby's Bar must have looked like an extension of Number One Court, Old Bailey. There were some serious faces there. I suppose we must have looked terrifying to any innocent bystander who'd just popped in for a drink. But we weren't out for bother. Far from it, this was Essex Boys at play, a sort of crooks' convention, and play we did.

It was the first time, really, that I'd had a chance to let my hair down and enjoy myself since Tony was killed. The island had many evocative memories of the good times we'd had there and in my mind I could see him standing there at the bar enjoying himself, unaware of what was to come. It seemed impossible that he wasn't around any more.

Anyway, it was now game on. The vodkas and bourbons were coming up in doubles and no one was paying. Poor old Joe was looking aghast at the sight of his profits disappearing down the necks of his mates from the smoke. So it was time to move on and let the rest of Playa de las Americas enjoy our company.

Danny lived out there full-time and led us round the best bars where he knew our little army would be welcome. We were treated like kings. We didn't have to pay for a thing. Danny's mates plied us with free booze in bar after bar, club after club, hour after hour. Each place we went into we formed a sort of magic circle, all these heavies shoving it down their throats like Armageddon was round the corner, as if we were inside a barbed wire fence like dangerous animals while ordinary holidaymakers just watched and wondered what the fuck was going on.

Everywhere we went, the bar owners knew in advance we were coming and, as we walked in, the bottle of vodka or Jack Daniel's was plonked down for us to get stuck into. It was the binge to end all binges. And our lot could drink.

But, one by one, even they fell by the wayside until there were just five of us left standing. We ended up in a pisshole of a club at about 8.30 the next morning after drinking right through the night. I was so pissed I can't remember what the place was called or where it was. I only know it was seedy, the sort of dive that attracts life's undesirables. By now we must certainly have ranked among them. There were gay boys, transsexuals, transvestites, all sorts dancing away. And us. Four severely mullered maulers from Essex. It all seemed like a right good laugh at the time and in a crap club like that and in our condition I suppose we had found the level we deserved. We wouldn't have done it sober.

Then it was time to snatch some sleep before doing it all again as we knew we surely would. We called a cab to get us, all bleary-eyed, back to our hotel for a few hours' kip. We packed in like sardines, two six-footers and two 17-stoners all shoved in one taxi and all as pissed as rats. The sun was high in the sky by now and I could barely open my eyes to look as we pulled up outside the marble entrance foyer of our hotel. We literally crawled out of the cab ... and I fell flat on my face. Then I crawled on my hands and knees through the foyer trying to make it to the lift and up to my room on the fifth floor. I couldn't even stand up long enough to push the lift button. The hotel doormen were looking on horrified at these four drunken hulks crawling and staggering past.

Without the use of the lift the only alternative was to climb the stairs. It felt like the north fucking face of the Eiger. I clambered slowly up to the first-floor landing. Then I got that terrible swirly feeling and just knew I had to puke. The only receptacle to hand was a rather splendid porcelain urn with a small palm growing in it. Uuuurgh! The technicolour yawn splashed all over it. I just hope it had some growing power!

I was woken up a few hours later by Phil who was ready for the off again. A livener of a spicy hot Bloody Mary with double vodka soon sorted the hangover. Then it was party time again. And that's how it went for the next four days, like a fucking mad drinking competition. We were going crazy. I know we must have been intimidating to outsiders but we weren't intent on harming anyone. I suppose being loud, lairy and rat-arsed would have been enough to ruin many a holiday.

That night, we all went for a paella at a seafood restaurant on the front in the better quarter of the island. About ten of us sat down to the biggest fucking plate of paella you've ever seen – lobster, prawns, mussels – lovely. Naturally, we needed a drink to wash it down. Plenty of vino and lager was being consumed. Then Phil spotted the yard of ale glass. He said, 'I bet you couldn't ...' He didn't need to finish the sentence.

I said to the barmaid, 'Right, love, fill it up ... with vodka.'

The others all jeered and shouted, 'You'll never drink that ...'

'You reckon?'

The waitress poured almost a whole bottle of Smirnoff blue label in the glass and topped it up with lemonade. Glug! glug! glug! I downed the fucking lot. The lads all cheered and then waited for me to fall over. Then someone called out, 'I've got some afters for you, Carl.'

What afters? An Ecstasy pill was put in my hand.

'Bet you won't take that.'

Full of booze and full of bravado and out for a good time whatever the cost, I swallowed it straight down. I was off my face on alcohol and now the pill started making me soppy. I had a big grin like a Cheshire cat on my face. I had an irresistible urge to do a moonie. So, quick as a flash, it was off with my shorts, off with my shirt, off with my pants and I was running along the promenade in the best part of Tenerife showing everything I'd got. The looks on the faces of all the upper-class diners in the different restaurants was a picture. One woman dropped her knife and fork. Another sat open-mouthed as I pranced along, then did a Tarzan roar through some palms and an Adam and Eve cover up of the naughty bits with a fig leaf. My lot were in fits.

And so it went on. I don't think Tenerife had seen a rampage like it. On the last night, we had a final monster session and I got back to the hotel at dawn soaking wet. I can't remember how. I don't know whether I'd been in the sea or in a pool but my clothes were ringing. The trouble was that my money was in my trouser pocket. In my drunken state, I decided to take the sodden peseta notes out and lay them on a small table on my hotel balcony to dry. So far so good. While they were wet they stayed put. But as soon as they dried, of course, they started fluttering in the breeze and took off. I looked up from the bed and saw thousands of pesetas floating off into the hotel car park and beyond. I rushed on to the balcony and grabbed what was left but most of my money was a goner. I thought about chasing it but realised that in the time it would take me to get downstairs it would be long gone in that stiff Canaries breeze. I thought, Fuck it, but never mind, I've had a blinding few days. But I've just doubled the cost in 30 seconds.

Perhaps, if there is any justice, the money was picked up by some of those folks whose holidays we messed up. I know for sure that a couple of people in our hotel left early because they were so pissed off with our drunken shenanigans. To them, I can only say sorry.

When we came to say goodbye to Joe, he looked us in the eye and said, 'You really are going, aren't you? Please say you are. I've been here for 18 years and I've never been involved in anything as mad as you lot.'

We said we'd had a great time and would do it all again one day.

He looked worried, like we might decide to stay on a bit. 'Tell you what,' he said, 'give us your flight time and I'll pick you up and take you to the airport and make sure you're on board when it takes off. I can't handle any more of you.'

Then he jokingly handed us our drinks bill for the four days, a whacking great £3,000. I said, 'You're kidding.'

Joe said, 'Tell you what, if you promise me you're definitely going home and won't be back I'll forget it.'

To the relief of Joe and the Tenerife Tourist Board, we were safely aboard our flight that afternoon.

10

Cheque Mate

In my game, we called it work, though it wasn't exactly in the mould of the nine-to-five, pin-striped brigade up from Surbiton on the 8.42. But it was work nonetheless, often with guns, knives and beatings as the tools of our trade. In this particular case, it was a bit of work involving £250,000 worth of travellers' cheques. Bent American Express travellers' cheques, to be precise, not quite hot but still pretty warm. It looked like being a good earner and I needed a reliable outlet to cash them up.

Tony Tucker was on the up and up in gangland then. He took some samples and they came good. They were accepted without question on a couple of trial runs and we were up and running. Now we needed the rest of the nicked cheques. The firm holding them wanted about £25,000 cash up front to secure the deal. Tony was the sort of guy who kept that amount of cash about the place. I decided to chip in as well to earn a bit of drinking money. We got the cash together and arranged a meet with the boss man at a farm in Essex. He turned up looking the business in a 20-grand Roller. But we hit a problem straight away – no travellers' cheques. A second geezer, due to be bringing them to the meet failed to show. Suddenly, a nice little job was looking a bit shaky. And that sort of thing did not please Tony Tucker. He'd got the serious hump. I wasn't happy because I'd brokered the package in the first place and didn't like being pissed about.

We set up another meet at the Thurrock Services area just off the M25 at the junction with the A13. But, again, the cheques failed to materialise. Now Tony was getting really irritated, and my credibility was being called into question. We decided that amateurs like that, failing to deliver on a deal, deserved punishment. Tony made up a fake parcel of cash, with genuine notes on the outside and cut paper inside, to pull off a sting that would teach them not to fuck with us. We tucked the cash into a bag so that it looked the real McCoy and arranged a third and, we hoped, final meet. But, again, the cheque gang failed to bring the goods. Now we were into three days' work with no return and Tony was steaming mad. When someone crossed Tony, he could be a fucking maniac. And he had a very, very short fuse which was already reaching explosion point. A fourth meet was set up but was cancelled at the last minute. Tony said, 'These fuckers are giving us the runaround, Carl.' Pat Tate was growling and that always spelt danger.

We decided there would be no more messing around on this deal. If they wouldn't bring the cheques to us, we'd go and take them – by force. We had managed to get hold of an address for the gang boss at Leytonstone in East London and headed there one morning four-handed and tooled up. No sign of anyone. The raid came to nothing.

But we weren't about to drop it. It had dragged on for weeks and had become a matter of underworld honour. It was important for our reputations that we got it sorted. So, next we fixed a meet at a pub in Woodford. This time, we really meant business. We went six-handed in a big Shogun 4x4 and a BMW, tooled up of course. I was dressed head to toe in my trademark black and topped off with a baseball cap like the police marksmen wear. We looked like a fucking commando unit. It was dark and we sat just out of sight across the road waiting for the action.

The geezer we wanted to see, Pete Willis, arrived and went into the pub with another couple of blokes. They came out again minutes later ready to talk turkey with us. But they didn't get a chance. Tony and Pat went steaming across the car park and waded into them. One of them was cut straight away, and was pouring blood. I don't know whether it was Tony or Pat's blade. We had planned to take the fuckers quietly without causing a scene in a public place. But already it was getting out of hand.

Crash! Tony hit one of them with a right-hander. The bloke sprawled backwards across the bonnet of a pub customer's car and set the alarm off. It started wailing and house lights started flickering on. Blokes were screaming and yelling as we were trying to catch them and there was a right old mêlée going on which was certain to attract the Old Bill.

Tony said we needed to grab one of the geezers and shove him in the back of the Shogun so we could do the business somewhere less conspicuous. By now, another couple of car alarms were ringing out, triggered off by the rumpus. Time was getting short.

I grabbed one of the cheque gang and tried to manhandle him in through the rear door of the Shogun. He started wriggling like a fucking rabbit and then he slipped out of his coat and did a runner into the night. I was left standing there with the coat in my hands watching the geezer disappear into the darkness screaming in terror. I had to laugh.

I said to Tony and Pat, 'Come on, it's all gone belly up, we've got to get out of here before the rozzers arrive.' In seconds, we were gone. But Tony's fury was reaching detonation point. Willis and this firm were marked men. The bond of friendship that had been forged between Willis and Pat Tate while they were in prison together was out of the window. Tony decided Willis must be punished for his piss-taking by way of an instant 'fine' – so his car was nicked and offered to me for free. I said, 'No, I don't really want it.'

Tony said, 'He's bounced you, Carlton, you have it. We'll fine the bastard.'

This was Tucker's Law and I went along with it. This was around the time when I noticed that Tony's drug habits were making him increasingly violent, irrational and even more dangerous than usual and the whole atmosphere around our firm was getting scary. I'd always been involved in a bit of ducking and diving to earn a few bob, but now things were coming on top. There was danger in the air.

Willis had become an obsession with Tony. One night, he and Pat went round to his flat out of their brains on drugs, dragged him into the bedroom, laid him on the bed and shoved a gun into his mouth. They were laughing as they played a cruel game of Russian roulette with Tony's finger on the trigger clicking away and Willis out of his nut shitting himself waiting for the bang. Tony was saying, 'We're going to blow your head off, you fucker,' and calling him all sorts of names. He was so terrified it took him months to recover. He knew he'd been lucky. With the mood Tony was in, Willis knew that if he'd fucked up he wouldn't get a second chance.

I know he'd inflicted the same kind of terrifying punishment on Craig, his supposed buddy, a couple of times as well. He'd threatened to blow his brains out and told him he'd be off the firm if he didn't get his act together. Tony had become a savage and brutal man without a stop button to halt his descent into becoming a fully-fledged, uncontrollable, drug-induced psychopath.

I'd tried to reason with Tony. When he'd told me about the things he'd done to Willis and to Craig, I told him, 'That's not really right, Tony, you don't torture and terrorise people for the fun of it.'

I am a great believer that if you pull out a gun, you intend to use it. It's not a toy, not a plaything for sadists. But my words fell on deaf ears. Tony, Pat and Craig were hell-bent on making Willis suffer for the bodged-up travellers' cheques.

They started going into his flat, robbing him, frightening the life out of him over and over, like they were enjoying it.

Because they were all jacking up and snorting stuff, there was no reasoning with them. They were using everything – crack cocaine, freebase coke, Special K (as ketamin was called), some lignocaine – anything they could shove up their noses or stick in their arms that gave them a buzz. I didn't want to get into conflict with Tony. I regarded him as my best mate and I supplied a lot of the muscle for his doors. We both did well out of it. But I was getting increasingly edgy about the way things were going.

Then Pat got shot and the temperature was getting even higher. I remember Tony turning up late at a big gangsters' party at Phil's snooker hall in Dagenham and saying that Willis had put one in Pat's arm with a pistol, causing a nasty but not life-threatening injury. Our first concern was that Pat was in serious trouble with the prison authorities because he was still on parole from his last sentence and any suggestion that he was mixed up in any sort of villainy and he'd be back inside so fast his feet wouldn't touch the deck. And that would be a key member of the firm out of action.

Tony said Pat had been shot by someone hiding in the bushes of the garden at his bungalow near Basildon. He'd been in the bathroom with his little boy when someone had rattled off two shots in quick succession and Pat had instinctively put up an arm to protect himself and the child and the bullet had smashed into his arm and out the other side.

Although Tony had no evidence as to who had fired the shots, he said, 'I know it's that bastard Willis.' I asked Tony if he was certain, because there would be a list of people who might take a pop at Pat. He snapped, 'Of course I'm sure, that little fucker has definitely done it. He's going to pay for this.' It was a sinister prediction that people knew would soon become reality.

It brought the party to a rapid close. Tony was gutted. I was gutted. Nobody felt like partying any more. Normally, these underworld shindigs are a right good laugh. Locked doors, coded entry only, no strangers allowed. This was gangland letting its hair down away from prying eyes. Now people were leaving early, drinks half-finished, and the only topic of conversation was Pat's shooting. And, of course, what Tony's next move would be.

We visited Pat in hospital the next day. He was surprisingly chirpy for someone who'd just stopped a .38 bullet. He, too, was certain that the would-be assassin was Willis. Tony said, 'Right, find him. I want all the stops pulled out. Find the fucker. He's done Pat and he's going to die.'

I was a little bit half-hearted about starting a big search. I knew that Pat and Tony had both terrorised Willis and that this was probably the frightened victim striking back on the basis that he must get them before they finish him or life would be a nightmare for ever and a day. I could imagine how he felt. I know I would have struck back as well.

I didn't argue with Tony because it was pointless but I knew more bloodshed was on the agenda for the Essex Boys. I wasn't far wrong.

A couple of days later, Tony and Craig stormed into Willis's home at Leigh-on-Sea and Willis was hiding in the garden, gun in hand. He started firing at them, panic stricken, in broad daylight. Then he made a run for his life. Tony was quickly on the phone to me screaming, 'The bastard, I'm going to kill him when I get hold of him.'

I said, 'Well, why do you keep going round there? He's shit-scared of you.'

Tony was having none of it. 'I'm going to kill him. I'm going to take everything he's got.'

I thought to myself, This is madness, absolute fucking madness. I'd got my security work going on in London and a few little things on the go on my own and I could see this Willis business and Tony's manic obsessions bringing it on top for me. I wasn't about to ditch our friendship but I didn't want to be put on offer for something that wasn't really my concern. It was getting silly.

I thought I might be able to pour a bit of soothing oil on these troubled waters by seeing Willis and having a chat. He admitted straight away that he *was* the gunman who'd shot Pat. But he was in a terrible state. He was sobbing down the phone and said that his family had been threatened and were too frightened even to step outside their door. He said, 'I've got people who say you are a good person, Carlton, and you won't hurt me.'

I told him I'd try and do what I could behind the scenes to take the heat off. But with the mood Tony was in, I was making no promises.

We started going into hospital regularly to see Pat. By now, he was off the general ward and in a side room on his own. Well, I've never seen anything like it in a hospital. Pat was getting regular supplies of coke and crack and holding wild drug parties that the hospital authorities were too scared to stop. And to top it all, he'd even got a brass in there for sex. Tony had hired the escort girl at £500 a day and she more or less moved in to Pat's room. He was a man with a big sexual appetite and the girl earned her money the hard way, if you get my drift.

I walked in one afternoon and there was a crowd all laughing and joking. Then I saw Craig in the adjoining bathroom washing up some cocaine to turn it into rocks to smoke as crack. The brass was lying on the bed beside Pat, looking like she'd had a hit of something as well. And, to top it all, he'd got a shooter in a drawer beside the bed. I couldn't believe my eyes. Tony saw the expression on my face and burst into uncontrollable laughter. That was it. Everyone started laughing, like it was all one big joke, including Pat, a man on parole from jail in a hospital room with drugs and a gun. Talk about chancing your arm, even if it has got a bullet hole in it.

I could see the madness of it all. It was chaotic. Tony had lost it. They'd all lost it. But I don't work like that. I rounded on Craig and his crack factory. 'You're off your fucking heads.'

I could see the crack, the most addictive of all forms of cocaine, a plastic bottle to smoke it, I could see powdered cocaine, pills, pipes, puff, all sorts. Some of the people had been partying there all night. Tony had slept on the floor. I couldn't believe this could happen in a National Health hospital. I couldn't believe the nursing staff and doctors would tolerate it. But I suppose, on reflection, who's going to risk a good hiding by grassing up a hard-looking bunch like that?

A nurse came in while me and my pal were on the visit and must have clocked what was going on. She didn't say anything. I just muttered excuses about visiting a friend and turned to my mate and said, 'Come on, we're out of here. This is crazy.' I looked at the others all out of their skulls and said, 'What are you fucking doing? You are well out of order.' I thought they were putting everyone in jeopardy by their stupidity. I like a laugh, but this was sheer lunacy.

My predictions were right. Early the next day the police steamed in and nicked Pat in his room, in possession of the handgun, a bag of pills, an ounce of puff and cocaine. The prostitute was still in business and standing by Pat's bed. They'd been shagging on and off all night in a public hospital. You can't do that.

That's when the craziness of it all hit me like a ton of bricks. They weren't just out of control, they were uncontrollable. They'd terrified the hospital staff in the belief that they were now above the law, that they were the Essex untouchables. No one is above the law, be it the law of the land or the law of the jungle. Now the law had hit back with a full-scale armed raid on Pat's room. Someone had obviously tipped them off about the gear and gun, and they gave the operation the 'Full Monty' treatment. They knew about Pat's reputation and his associates and took no chances. Tony and Craig also put their hands up to some of the drug charges which was only fair because they'd brought most of the stuff in. Pat claimed he never knew the gun had been brought in, but the cops had enough to get him banged up again straight away in a Category A high-security prison hospital wing.

In the meantime, I was getting more calls from Willis. He was in bits. I felt really sorry for him. He'd been under more pressure than any man should be asked to endure. While Pat was in hospital, Willis had got hold of a shooter and had hidden in the car park waiting for Tony to come out to have another crack at him. It came to nothing, but Willis was still tearing his hair out with worry. He was cracking up.

I knew he was reaching the end of the line when he phoned one day, in tears, and said, 'I want to ask you a big, big favour.'

I said, 'It depends on what you want.'

I could barely believe it when he said, 'I want you to kill me.'

I was flabbergasted.

He repeated, 'Would you shoot me, Carlton? I can't go on living like this. I haven't got the bottle to kill myself ... will you do it for me?'

I said, 'You can't ask me to do that. You can't ask that of any person.' It was like he was having a dog put down. No way was I going to be part of that. I knew from the terror in his voice that this was no idle request. This man wanted to die, and he wanted to make me the executioner. I told him there wasn't the remotest possibility of it taking place and told him to go on the run, go and hide somewhere safe, until I had a chance to put in a word for him. Then he wanted a meet.

He came to my house in Brentwood. I have never, in my whole life, seen such a broken wreck of a man. He was trembling non-stop, shaking from head to toe. And he still had the gun tucked under his coat. He was togged up in a bulletproof vest. I knew I had to be careful. We walked through to the kitchen to talk, knowing that if he was as totally unhinged as I believed, he might have a go at me. I undid my shirt.

'Look, I'm not carrying anything. You are safe here.' A visible look of relief swept across his haggard face. But still he was nervous, cautious to the extreme.

'You might be setting me up.'

I said, 'Look, I'm a man of my word. I'm trying to calm things down. I don't want to see anyone killed.'

We talked and talked for over an hour. He was like a condemned man. Then I saw him twiddling the revolver under his jacket. I said, 'Don't be fucking silly. What are you going to do? I'm not going to hurt you.'

He said despairingly, 'Carlton, I just don't know who to trust.'

All this grief, I thought, over a bit of work that had gone wrong, a few miserable travellers' cheques. 'Right,' I said, 'you've got to get off the manor, get right away 'til it blows over. In the meantime, I'll talk to the people who are after you.'

Finally, I was able to persuade him to trust me, to let me handle Tony, Craig and Pat. I even managed to get him to hand me the revolver, just for a look, of course. It did flash through my mind that I could now turn it on him and call Tony. But this poor bastard had suffered enough. He stayed agitated until he'd got the shooter safely back in his custody, and then he calmed down a bit. He seemed to realise that I wasn't about to turn him in to his enemies. It was one of the tensest moments of my life. Here was a man, frightened of me, apprehensive in the extreme, sitting with his finger on the trigger of a loaded revolver and I had managed to coax him into handing it over. It was a personal achievement I was proud of. But the situation still left Willis a broken man, a nervous wreck watching every shadow.

It wasn't long before he was picked up by police and charged with the shooting of Pat Tate. He was probably safer on remand in jail than wandering about Essex ducking bullets.

With Pat also out of the way for a while, the likelihood of another shoot-out diminished. But Pat wasn't a man to lie down and roll over, even though he was back in the slammer. Me and Tony visited him regularly. Had he learned anything from the hospital drug bust? Not a bit of it. He was still phoning up members of the firm asking them to smuggle drugs inside prison for him.

I went once with Tony and he had drugs hidden in a book.

'What the fuck are you doing?' I asked.

'Oh, Pat wants them.'

These two guys really sparked off each other. Together, they were a nightmare. Alone, Tony was a different bloke. And while Pat was inside, I could see the old Tony I knew and loved coming back again. Funny, generous, considerate. Except for the drugs. That's one thing he couldn't kick.

I got a panic telephone call from his girlfriend one night. She was screaming and crying.

'What's the matter, what's up?'

She sobbed, 'Tony's just broken a needle in his arm.'

He'd had trouble looking for a vein to inject a fix and had stuck the pin in a bone and snapped it clean in two. She said, 'He's walking round with it squirting blood everywhere and he won't go to hospital. He'll kill me if he knows I've called you.'

I knew what sort of needle he used, a big fucker like the type I had for injecting steroids. This was serious.

'Tell him he must get to a hospital or he will die,' I said. 'Don't take no for an answer.'

Tony eventually agreed and doctors surgically removed the jammed needle.

'Tony,' I said later, 'it's time you and me went away for a holiday.'

I told my partner Denny that I was going away on a spot of business, collecting an overdue debt in Spain and I'd ring her from the Costa del Sol. Then I went and picked up my mistress, Lynn, met up with Tony and we caught a plane to Malta and booked into the Holiday Inn. Tony was happy to chip in for half of the cost because he really needed to get away, he needed to escape from drugs and the tension of the whole Essex gangland scene. I could see he was suffering withdrawal symptoms but he was trying hard to find himself again away from the pills, powders and needles. We went out for meals and drinks and he seemed to be coping. But I knew he was in deep trouble. The veins in his arms were dotted with injection scars and had turned a sort of grey colour. He wasn't the man I had first met, he'd lost his zap. But I was big on his case trying to get him off drugs, to clean him up, and with Pat's influence no longer there I reckoned I could get the old Tony back. With Willis banged up, too, on firearms charges, I hoped the volatile situation of the past few weeks was now subsiding. It was a good holiday overall and Tony showed definite signs of improvement. Then we arrived back at Heathrow airport and Craig was there to meet him in the arrivals lounge. And what's he got? A fucking bag of gear. I was fucking livid. I walked out of the toilet where they were jacking up on Charlie shaking my head in despair. I'd been trying to save a friend's life and all my work was being undone in seconds. It became patently obvious that Tony didn't really want to come off drugs or his addiction was so deep-rooted he just couldn't kick the habit. And it was to get worse in the run-up to the triple murders at Rettendon. Smack, ketamin, crack and Nubane were all regularly on the menu at his drug binges in unlimited quantities. The Nubane did, in fact, help to calm him down. It's a morphine-based painkiller which seemed to soothe his temperament and he was able to get back to a bit of training at the gym.

Even though he was being dragged down by drug addiction, he was conscious of the need to work out to keep himself in shape. He seemed to be making a big effort to clean himself up. He'd also taken up with a teenage girlfriend, Donna Garwood, which really surprised me because I thought his relationship with Anna Whitehead was really strong, especially when they moved from Chafford Hundred to a mansion of a place at Fobbing called Brynmount Lodge.

Then Pat came out of jail again. He'd done another year for breaking his parole and offences connected to the hospital bust. That was nothing to a man like Pat Tate. He'd originally been sentenced to six years inside for robbing a Happy Eater restaurant and possessing cocaine. He'd got into a row over the bill and he and a girlfriend decided to help themselves to the takings. When he was remanded to Chelmsford Prison by Billericay Magistrates, he vaulted over the side of the dock, shrugged off the efforts of six police officers to hold him down and dashed from the court and roared off on a waiting high-powered motorbike. He vanished to Spain and stayed in hiding on the Costa del Sol for a year. But he then made the mistake of visiting friends in neighbouring Gibraltar and was promptly nicked by the British authorities and returned to jail in the UK. He served four of his six years, leaving prison a bitter and angry man in the grip of hard drugs and a racing certainty to be in trouble again in double-quick time. So it proved. He was back behind bars within 12 months.

We hired a huge stretch limo to meet him when he came out after his breach of parole sentence was over and waited outside Whitemoor Prison in Cambridgeshire. It must have looked like a welcoming party from the Basildon branch of the Mafia. I'm sure it didn't go unnoticed by the prison authorities or police. Pat had not used his time inside to clean up his act. Just the opposite, in fact. He'd put pressure on various people, including Tony, to slip him drugs, including heavy-duty steroids, on visits. Me and Tony had argued over it. I told him, 'Don't put me in that situation. What anyone else does is their business but I think it's stupid.'

Anyway, Tony totally ignored me and I saw him slip a

syringe and some drugs to Pat right under my nose as we were chatting in the visiting area. It was so quick the screws and the CCTV didn't pick up on it. He was a big, awesome, powerful man, 18-and-a-half stone with a big personality to match. He was much admired in underworld circles and his escape from the magistrates court was already written in to Essex gangland folklore. I suspect the screws were a bit in awe of him. He was a man to be feared, a man who could sort out problems, so I think maybe he had his uses inside. He had lots of clout among black and white prisoners alike, so I reckon the screws thought he could oil the wheels for them. I think that was the way they looked on him.

So he strolled out through the gates of Whitemoor an hour-and-a-half later than scheduled, like a conquering fucking hero, fit, tanned and as handsome as ever. The illusion was soon shattered. There was all the back-slapping, the hugging, the kissing, then the champagne corks popped and Pat was back in town. Within minutes of driving off, someone had pulled out a big bag of gear and they were all at it again. I thought, Oh shit, this is never ending. I'm just banging my head against the wall.

I'd tried to help Tony. Now I knew my cause was lost. Big Pat was a malign influence that was to see Tony back on the slippery slope within days. It started with a massive gangland party at Tony's house. Not that I didn't like Pat. He was a terrific character. But he seemed to mesmerise Tony.

As soon as he was out Tony lent him his black Porsche. Pat was swanning round Southend in it, boozed up, bird at his side, when he got involved in a smash and was pulled by the police. Not only was he out of his head, the car contained several gun shells belonging to Tony, which he held legally as a member of a gun club, so he was bringing a load of shit down on us unnecessarily. I was with Tony when Pat phoned and I was furious. I thought this was the height of disrespect and I wanted to tell him so.

'You are bang out of order,' I said, 'you just don't do that sort of thing.'

Tony was visibly shocked, as if I shouldn't be talking to Pat like that. Another waste of breath. Next, Pat's gone out and bought an identical black Porsche, same year, and they've started their crazy 140mph races up the A127.

So the madness went on. It takes a lot to shock me, but what I saw the day I drove out to see Tony's house at Fobbing knocked me sideways. He'd had a row with the kitchen fitter, a one-time mate called Jeff, and had called him back to finish some work on the luxury kitchen. And I do mean luxury — big, top of the range Aga, the bollocks, over ten grand's worth. He'd had Jeff back time and time again but still wasn't satisfied.

'Here,' he said, 'I got hold of Jeff last night.' He had a sadistic smirk on his face.

'Oh yeah,' I said, 'how is he?'

Tony said, 'Come and see,' and took me outside. There was poor Jeff chained up, cut and bruised, in the dog kennel with the Alsatians. Jeff crawled out on his hands and knees and Tony laughed. It was one of the most humiliating sights I've ever seen a fellow man endure. Jeff had spent the whole night and half the day crawling round in the piss and the shit, sleeping with the Alsatians, drinking and eating out of their food bowls.

'I had to teach him not to fuck me about,' Tony told me.

I said, 'For fuck sake, let him go. That's inhuman and degrading.'

Tony just laughed again and said, 'Yeah, I know.'

11

The Benn Years

I don't frighten easily, but Nigel Benn once scared me shitless during a training jaunt in the Canary Islands. Not many people know this, but as well as being a world-class boxer, Nigel is also an ace car driver. Good enough, in fact, to have succeeded at rally or even Grand Prix driving.

Me and Tony had flown to Tenerife with him, as mates as well as minders, as he got into serious training for one of his big title fights. The object was to get a bit of altitude work into him and we all piled into a BMW 320i and set off up the main mountain on the island, 7,000ft-high Mount Teide.

We were all chatting away, enjoying the experience, admiring the views as we climbed higher and higher until we were among low cloud. It was spectacular. Then suddenly – Wham! – Nigel had spun the car full circle on a handbrake turn on the side of the mountain with a 500ft drop only feet away. I remember both me and Tony going 'Aargh' as we thought we were goners. We stopped in a screech of brakes and a cloud of dust.

Nigel was laughing his head off. It was his idea of a joke. But we had all thought the Dark Destroyer was about to destroy us. I said, 'You wanker, Nigel!'

We looked over the side of the mountain road and it was a big, big drop. I had visions of the newspaper headlines back home saying BOXING CHAMP DIES IN MYSTERY MOUNTAIN PLUNGE.

The next time we went up from the training camp we had Ray, one of Nigel's sparring partners, with us. Me and Tony half knew what to expect. We were gripping tight as we wound up the mountain road. Up, up, up. I thought, You're not going to do it, are you? We were about as high as you can get before the road runs out. Then the smirk came over Nigel's face. Wallop! He spun the motor 360 degrees again. Me and Tony both looked at Ray. His mouth was open and his eyes were popping out of his head.

'What the fuck?' he shouted.

Another knock-out laugh to Nigel. But I suppose it wouldn't have pleased his promoter, agent or insurance company to know that Britain's favourite fighter was dicing with death up a Spanish mountain. How would that have looked if we'd had a crash and ended up dead or badly injured? Someone saying, 'It was just his party trick, done for a laugh,' would sound a bit of a sorry explanation. But that was Nigel, as fearless behind the wheel of a car as he was in the ring.

MUSCLE

I don't know when he decided it would be a laugh to spin a Beamer half-way up a mountain but he wasn't a fool and must have felt confident that he had everything under control. I did worry, though, that one day he would overcook it with one of his stunts and end up badly hurt in a wrecked motor.

They were good days with Nigel. I have the greatest respect for him as a fighter and as a human being, and we remained good friends through thick and thin. And we did have some traumas.

We regularly flew out to the Tenerife training camp with him and went through the motions of top-level, high-pressure workouts with him. I say 'through the motions' because it's only when you try it that you realise what a tough regime these guys set themselves. They make it look so easy. Then they are superbly fit specimens of manhood. Me and Tony were big, muscley bodybuilders who could hold our own any day of the week in a nightclub ruckus, but we couldn't hold a light to Nigel when it came to stamina, speed and supreme fitness.

He once invited me to try a workout session on the pads in the gym. I'd seen Nigel do it and Tony do it. So I got gloved up and set about knocking seven bells out of the pads. No warm up, just straight in, whack, whack, whack. But I was too big, too musclebound, and within a few minutes a searing pain went through the ligaments in my shoulder. I'd ripped a ligament just under my arm. It hurt like fuck and taught me a valuable lesson – being fit and being musclebound are two very different things. I tried running with Nigel at high altitude on the mountain. I knew my left leg wasn't strong after the car accident so I volunteered to do a downhill session of about a mile with Nigel while Tony drove the car. When we stopped, I was shot away. My whole 17-stone body was shaking in convulsions. I had difficulty breathing. My muscles were a burden, not a help. 'Oh, yeah, yeah, that was great, Nigel,' I gasped.

After that, it was strictly the gym for me, weights and bars, fuck those hills.

Nigel always paid for the villa in Tenerife and we bought our own plane tickets. We were pleased and proud to be there. If he needed us, we were never far away. Nigel kept himself to himself most of time while he was in training mode but occasionally he went out and found himself being mobbed by fans. He was a top international sporting figure and recognised the world over. Mostly people liked him. We were always there to ensure no one got too enthusiastic. He liked to relax playing records as guest DJ at Bobby's Bar on the holiday island. It was cool. The faces of unsuspecting holidaymakers when they walked through the door and saw hot-shot boxer Nigel at the turntable was a picture.

I remember one visitor from Manchester going up to him and saying, 'Hey, you don't half look like Nigel Benn.'

Nigel smiled and said, 'No, mate, just a lookalike.'

A lot would have said, 'I *am* Nigel Benn,' and revelled in the adulation. But not Nigel. He liked the quiet life. They were good times away from the tensions of London and Essex.

Tony's death hit Nigel badly. Though he was unaware of Tony's criminal activities, he could see a ton of bad publicity heading his way as newspapers and TV explored the relationship between top boxer and murdered drug-dealer. He was shocked by the information coming out about the criminal activities of Tony and the other boys. He could hardly believe this was the same Tony Tucker he knew and liked. He had planned to have Tony's name emblazoned across his boxing shorts for all to see in the next fight as a public token of their friendship. He was advised – don't. His management could see that even in the tough world of professional boxing, to have links with a major drug-dealer, a man who had walked you out through the crowds at all your top fights, was certain to bring much unwelcome publicity.

Tony's death was principally being linked to the death of policeman's daughter Leah Betts and with Raquel's nightclub in Basildon where she got the Ecstasy tablet that had killed her and which was under the control of Tony and his firm. To have been seen supporting Tony Tucker would have been professional suicide for Nigel in that current climate.

It was time for the muscle to back off from the boxing champ. Nigel experienced his first major defeat, at the hands of Sugar Ray Malinga, in Newcastle, on the very first occasion he walked out to the ring without Tony and me beside him, in March 1996. He had phoned me a few days earlier and said, 'You will be there to walk me out, won't you?'

I said I would, but I had reservations, both for Nigel and for me.

'I really want you there,' he said, 'I'll call you to confirm.'

It was my birthday on the night of the fight. I thought, I can cancel my party, Nigel is more important. We were still good friends, despite all that was still going on in connection with the murders, and I thought I should be there. I sat and waited by the phone. I never heard another word. I was hurt by it. I thought I had been ditched at the last minute because of the fear of more bad publicity. I sat and watched the fight at home and, for the first time ever, I wanted Nigel to get beaten. He did.

But afterwards, I discovered that the silence was nothing to do with Nigel. He said his management had asked a secretary to do it but she had forgotten.

I was back at his side walking him ringside for the two fights against Steve Collins. He lost them both. And the glory days were over.

But we'd had some real good times along the way. I have many fond memories of the excitement, the buzz, of a big fight night as we walked Nigel out and the crowds parted to let him through, his minders at his side, millions watching on TV. I remember being ringside with Nigel at Wembley on the night Frank Bruno won that great fight against Oliver McCall. We were all ecstatic. Nigel was one of the first to climb in the ring to hug him and congratulate him. Great scenes.

We got back to the dressing room and Nigel discovered that he'd lost one of his hand-made gold and diamond Cartier ear studs in the excitement. He said, 'It's got to be in the ring. Quick, Carl, go and look for it.'

Look for it? It was bedlam out there, jubilant Bruno fans were thronging the arena, thousands and thousands of them. Nevertheless, because Nigel was worried about his poxy gold earring me and Tony started clambering our way back towards the ring. Talk about swimming against the tide. We were climbing over people, under people, over seats, over barriers and finally made it into the square. Amazingly, we spotted the glistening diamond among all the feet, undamaged, and I was down on my hands and knees to scoop it up. Then we had to repeat the operation, battling through the crowds yet again, to return the earring to Nigel. He took one look and said, 'Thanks, Carl, I never thought I'd see that again.'

I loved the fight game. And to be as close to the action as I was with Nigel was a fantastic thrill. I loved all the razzmatazz of walking him out from the dressing room, through the cheering crowds, hearing the music blasting out, feeling so proud when he won that I'd have big tears in my eyes. I stood with him when he peed blood after some of the tougher battles, caused by excessive punishment to his kidneys.

After a fight, if he was OK, we'd usually get changed and showered and head off for a club somewhere. It was amazing how Nigel could stand up to a fearsome battering in the ring, then within a couple of hours be ready to go out partying. He knew a lot of people in the nightclub business and we'd often have a club to ourselves, courtesy of the management.

He was an idol in clubland. We'd drink and dance and Nigel would DJ his way through the night, sometimes 'til 6.00 or 7.00 in the morning. That was his favourite way of unwinding. He was good, too. And he'd always manage to find some great funk and soul tracks to keep the punters happy. It was amazing, really. One minute trading punches in the ring with some of the toughest geezers in the world, next minute chilling out over a turntable in a nightclub.

He was professional enough to be able to choose a whole different style of music for different clubs in different parts of the country. Up North, more traditional stuff; London more funky, up-to-date stuff, a lot of good black singers. He even talked once of turning pro on the DJ scene when he retired from boxing. We were going to get a road show together and go on tour round the UK, or even abroad if we could get the bookings. He really fancied that lifestyle. But he had to knock that idea on the head when his twin babies came along. It wouldn't have been fair to Carolyne.

Nigel decided to honour a promise he'd made to do a DJ gig at Raquel's despite a wave of bad publicity over drug-dealing and Leah Betts's death. He turned up; very few punters did. It proved to be the last waltz for Raquel's. The club shut down for ever the following Friday.

Then Nigel got involved in a spot of bother with his former best mate Ray Sullivan which put him in court and dramatically changed his life for ever. It happened while the two of them were up at Legends club in the West End. I was working elsewhere at the time, so I never knew exactly what happened.

I had a call from Nigel saying this and that had gone off, there had been a fight, but he wasn't bothered about it interrupting his training schedule for the Steve Collins rematch and he wanted me to go to Tenerife with him as usual. Although the police in London were investigating the incident at Legends, I think some sort of deal was done whereby he wasn't charged right away to enable him to carry on training for the next six weeks. He was a big-name fighter, big box office, huge Sky TV rights, million-dollar man. The cops, apparently, had talks with Nigel's management team and agreed to let the fight go ahead because there was so much tied up in it. It was another sell-out fight at Manchester Arena and, once again, Nigel had packed them in, 8,500 punters. The public fucking loved him.

I was a bit disappointed that Nigel hadn't phoned me when he went out to Legends and got into that bust-up. The whole business probably wouldn't have happened. Carolyne had said to him to ring me. She told him, 'Get Carlton to make sure you are all right.' She always felt he was safe when he was with me. And he was. I always watched his back. I protected him. Because he was such a high-profile character, he always attracted attention, wherever he went, and not always the right sort of attention. There were girls who wanted to get hold of him to get him into bed and then sell the story to the *News of the World* or some other tabloid; then there were blokes who wanted to pick fights with him to prove how hard they were. He was there for the taking, an up-front, high-profile, high-publicity value, multi-millionaire, and a nice guy to boot, and he needed protection. I used to warn him how dangerous some of these gold-digger girls could be. However tempted he might be, however pretty the woman, I always said, 'Don't even think about it, Nige.' I really hate those slappers who sleep with someone famous and then go running to the newspapers. They are the lowest of the low. Cheap slags.

Everybody thought I was his minder, his bodyguard. But I wasn't. I was his friend. OK, I just happened to be a minder and a bodyguard, but I was at Nigel's side because I liked him and cared about him. I think I can honestly say we were soul mates. Walking a top boxer out to a big televised fight, like Eubank or Collins, might seem glamorous and I did enjoy it, but we were there to do a serious job. You never knew when a nutter might push out of the crowd, out of that sea of bodies, and have a go. Or even well-wishers going to give him a friendly pat might accidentally catch his eye with a finger, or a ring, and you've got a multi-million-pound match off because your fighter has accidentally injured an eye. Protection came in many ways.

So the bombshell dropped when Nigel was eventually nicked for attacking Ray Sullivan. No one seemed to know what was behind it all. Nigel just wasn't a violent man away from the boxing ring. Apparently it was all to do with something that had happened years earlier when Nigel was with Sharron and Ray Sullivan was with her sister. Nigel and Sharron's relationship was volatile, explosive.

Ray was Nigel's best mate, like a brother. We used to be with them at boxing matches and saw there was something special about their relationship. They were inseparable. Nigel thought more of Ray than he did of his own brothers. Ray went with him to a training camp in Los Angeles to prepare for a big fight, before I ever started walking him out with Tony on fight nights.

Later, he found out that his best mate, the man he trusted more than anyone in the world, had made a pass at his girlfriend and expressed his undying love. I think it must have been Sharron who told him, maybe out of spite during another of their blazing rows. Not surprisingly, Nigel got the hump. Ray, a bit of a playboy and lady-killer, hadn't denied it. So there was a big falling out. Nigel was badly affected mentally, he felt he had been betrayed, and it started to affect his fighting abilities. To this day, it still eats him up.

It exploded that night at Legends. There was a fight. Ray got a really good hiding. That might have been the end of it, except that Ray decided to go public and had his photo splattered all over the *Sun* with a big story saying how Nigel had beaten him up. The hospital photo showed Ray's tubes and clips and medical apparatus all pulled out on display to make it look worse than it was. He said he was going to take out a civil action against Nigel for damages. Then a lot of people started to turn their backs on Nigel. Ray was quite well liked around the club scene and now a lot of people had it in for Nigel and were slagging him off big time behind his back. They thought he was just a bully-boy boxer who'd smacked Ray for no reason. Then Nigel was charged with causing GBH and was awaiting trial in court. Nigel was feeling the pressure and he came to me and said, 'Carlton, I need help.'

I was going out with him to clubs and seeing people just turn their backs. They said to me, 'Why are you sticking with him, he's just a thug?'

I told them it wasn't for me to say. I was a friend and friends stick by each other. I suggested to Nigel that he went public, like Ray had, and gave his side of the story. Then people might understand. But he wouldn't.

With the court hearing pending, it was probably the right decision. They might have considered it contempt of court.

So, Nigel wanted help. I said I would explain the situation to people if Nigel didn't want to talk about it. Gradually, they were saying, 'Oh yes, we can see why it happened.' Nevertheless, I stayed close by his side. There was still danger out there for the Dark Destroyer.

The trial started at Middlesex Guildhall Crown Court in May 1997 in a blaze of publicity. The prosecution claimed Nigel had smashed a glass ashtray in Ray's face in a savage and unprovoked attack. Nigel and Sharron's love-life came under scrutiny as the motive for the assault which led to Ray having 105 stitches in his face and nose. She said, 'Nigel had loads of affairs but I was always 100 per cent faithful.'

Nigel said Ray, who worked as a ticket agent, had tried to frame him over the attack at Legends to try to get damages. The jury believed him and he was cleared of all the serious charges that could have put him inside. The judge, though, did say he thought Nigel had brought the prosecution on himself and refused his £50,000 defence costs.

I had to smile as the cheers went up for Nigel from supporters in the public gallery. The clouds had been lifted. Nigel walked out of court with me at his side, and went down on his knees in front of new love Carolyne, who'd sat through every minute of the hearing listening to distressing evidence about the man she adored and his previous relationship with Sharron, and he told her the verdict had been 'in the Lord's hand'. Nigel had found religion and had become a born-again Christian.

But Nigel had other enemies apart from Ray, and there was talk of an attack. I stayed close to him. I was protecting him even when he didn't know I was protecting him. He'd got everything to lose. I'd got fuck all to lose. Then I got a phonecall offering me £100,000 to turn my back on him. There was a hit out on him, said the caller, and they wanted me out of the way. There was a firm out there prepared to take on a contract to kill him and they considered me the main obstacle. I said, 'Bollocks, if you do him, best you do me first. You'll have to go through me to get to him.' That was it as far as I was concerned. No one was going near Nigel Benn. The caller, who reckoned he was acting as an intermediary and was not involved in the actual hit, said, 'Oh, I didn't realise you felt so strongly.' I think the vibes I put out told them I meant what I said. I've got a reputation for being hard but fair, and a friend is a friend for ever to me. Perhaps my refusal to be bought off may even have saved Nigel's life.

By now, Ray had taken out a civil action against Nigel for £50,000 damages. It was always going to be a bitter and acrimonious fight. I stayed at a hotel with Nigel day and night for two weeks when the case came up. I was never more than a few yards away, I stayed close by in the same hotel, I had breakfast with him and Carolyne, I travelled to court by taxi with them, I gave up two weeks of my life for Nigel. On top of that, I was busy behind the scenes.

I helped Nigel as much as I could. I put myself right on offer, really. Everybody knew who I was and where I stood with Nigel. I was with him every day. Every time he came out of court, I was photographed beside him on the steps. The media attention was constant, we were followed everywhere, chased down the street by camera crews, the pressure became intense. But I never once considered giving up on him. After two weeks, the damages claim was thrown out. Life returned to some sort of normality, or as normal as life can be for a world-class middleweight boxer living in the full glare of publicity and his now very public minder.

We still managed to get away from the spotlight for a bit of touring and DJ work. Our trips took us to the North, to Scotland and all over England with Nigel paying all the expenses and giving me money from what he was earning. We had some more good times now the storms had passed.

Then came one of the greatest honours of my life – Nigel asked me to be one of his best men at his and Carolyne's wedding blessing, along with his brother John, and our friends Wayne and Simon. It was a great party, held at his luxury home in Beckenham, Kent, a couple of weeks after he and Carolyne had secretly got married at a register office. Everyone was in top hat and tails, there were loads of celebrity guests, a gospel choir, magazine photographers, and Carolyne had had a full-size boxing ring set up in the garden early that morning to have the blessing in. Everyone was expected to give a little speech and they were all saying what a great bloke Nigel was.

I had to be the silly one, of course. I stood up and started cursing the top hat I was being forced to wear like some poxy toff. Then I put my hand inside and pulled out a white rabbit and gave it to Carolyne. It went down a bomb. Then I told the guests that I'd done a big speech for everyone and you could see them groaning as I fumbled with a piece of paper. When I unfolded it, it was a plain bit of paper about 4ft square with just the word 'SPEECH' written on it. Big, yes, but short, too. Everyone fell about laughing. I did a few jokes and it was a real good laugh. I did the security at the party for Nigel as well as being best man but there was never likely to be any trouble. Who's going to kick off at a party thrown by Nigel Benn with guests like Lennox Lewis and half the top muscle from London? No, it was a good day, one of my great memories of the highs and lows in the life of a great boxer and a good friend.

One notable absentee was lovely Frank Bruno, who'd once been a mate of Nigel's but had remained friendly with Ray Sullivan and, with all the bad feeling still going on, was not on the guest list. It was a shame, really. Everyone loved Frank. Me and Tony had met him a few times around the fight scene and he was great value. When he knew Tony had been killed, he beckoned me over at a fight in Manchester and said, 'I'm really sorry.' You knew this was genuine, from the heart. We had a brief chat about Tony, though, of course, he knew nothing of Tony's criminal activities. Frank knew we were really good mates as well as a team and he could see I was shattered by the news. He just called me over to his ringside seat while Nigel was warming up, strictly spontaneous, no one had asked him to, and for a man of his stature to take time to do that left a lasting impression of him as a really decent human being.

I went into Legends one night, well before the murders, and he was there with his wife having a meal.

'Hello, Frank.'

'Hello, Carlton.'

I told him I was out celebrating my birthday and he stood up and got me a drink and wished me well. Then we had a sort of friendly wrestle. It was great, Carlton and a big grizzly bear.

Nigel and I still talk occasionally but that magic of a special relationship has gone. I'm pleased he's found religion. I think he needed it in order to find himself. I wish him well. He can rest assured that the little secrets I know will remain safe with me, even in this book. He's a knock-out bloke, if you'll pardon the pun.

12

Molls

The little blonde behind the bar at an Essex nightspot hadn't taken a blind bit of notice of me when I was just an ordinary punter. But the moment I turned up as the new doorman – tuxedo, bow-tie and bulging biceps – it all changed. Rapidly. It was as if I was wearing some magic aftershave or had undergone a Linford Christie lunchbox transplant. Half-way through the evening, she was slipping cute little smiles my way. With half-an-hour to go, she was suddenly wanting to know which was the best taxi firm to use to get her home. Never one to miss an opportunity I volunteered my services with a nonchalant, 'Oh, it's on my way home ... see you later.' It was, in fact, in the opposite direction. She was waiting in the car park beside my Granada Ghia when I left. The time-honoured formula, that aura of power and danger that some women seemed to find irresistible, had worked the oracle.

I'd gone from nondescript also-ran to macho man with the pulling power of a Ferrari in a matter of hours! I don't even know what the attraction is myself but, throughout the annals of crime, bad men have always attracted good women. And not so good women. Plenty of evil, manipulating bitches have joined the gold rush to become as dangerous and ambitious as their menfolk. No self-respecting gangster would be seen out partying without a dolly bird on his arm. They are as much a trophy of villainy as the Mercedes, the mansion and the yacht. Now, I don't have any of those. Just a comfortable flat tucked away on the edge of a small Essex village with a second-hand car and enough money for my everyday needs. Not because I haven't made a nice few bob over the years. No, I've had it but I've blown it, mostly on women. And I've thoroughly enjoyed it.

It all started with that little nightclub blonde who wanted a lift home. She made me realise that there is a lure about the world of muscle, the danger factor of gangland, that some women just cannot resist, from the famed white stiletto scrubbers of deepest Essex to society blue-bloods who really should have more sense. Been there, done those.

That first pull as a doorman was, in fact, a bit of a disaster. She was waiting, as agreed, in the car park and we headed off towards Wanstead Flats, where on a good night you can see 20 motors gently rocking away in the moonlight. But at the last minute, I changed my mind and headed off towards Becton, where a load of building work was going on and I'd spotted a neat little shagging spot when I was out there with a mate a few days earlier. We pulled into the half-finished cul de sac, flanked by partly-built homes, and I was happy we wouldn't be getting any unwanted company as we got down to business. I had to restrict the passion to 20 minutes because my ever-suspicious first wife, Karen, was at home asleep and expecting me home around 4.00am, the normal sort of clocking-off time in the club world.

The blonde was manic, and we'd got the motor steamed up in minutes. She was into all sorts of positions even the *Kama Sutra* never mentioned, and was really, really up for it. I hope I didn't disappoint her. I sneaked a glance at my watch as we neared the vinegar strokes. It told me we were running out of time and Cinders needed to make a dash for it before pumpkin time. I switched on the engine a few minutes later and slipped the Granada into gear. I needed a three-point turn to get me out and heading homewards. Forward, back, forward ... then straight down a mud-filled ditch left by the workmen. I got out and saw my rear wheels up in the air.

'Fuck it, fuck it, fuck it,' I shouted, 'it's all your fucking fault.'

Poor cow, it wasn't her fault at all. I knew I had to try to get out of this predicament or face the wrath of the long-suffering Karen. I trudged on to the building site and grabbed some scaffolding planks. I wedged them under the wheels and got back in the car. Vroom, we edged forward. We were on the move. Then I realised that I'd ended up with the front wheels on one side of the ditch and the back wheels on the other.

'Fuck it, fuck it, fuck it.'

Then out of nowhere came a voice and a torch heading my way. The site security man had been watching everything with some bemusement. Well, not totally everything, I hope.

'Need some help?' he asked.

'Never more,' I said.

So the pair of us collected up as many planks as we could and formed a sturdy bridge under the motor, revved her up and away we went. The blonde got the quickest drop-off in history and I crept into my home and washed the mud and crap off my clothes and shoes.

'You're late, anything wrong?' came a sleepy voice from the bedroom.

'You'll never believe it but ...' and the excuse factory was rolling one out. This time, I said, some lunatic had swerved in front of me and forced me into a ditch and I'd had to get help pushing it out. She swallowed it that time. And the next. And the next. But after seven years of living together, one child and a thousand excuses for the late nights, for the lipstick smudges and the lingering perfume, for sometimes never coming home at all for days on end, Karen finally had enough and kicked me out.

But I knew by then, as I was drawn deeper and deeper into gangland and more dependent on the use of steroids, there was this dangerous chemistry at work which made pulling new women absurdly easy. I'd seen them flocking round the hard-cases I knew, big Pat Tate being a classic example, like moths to the candle flame, and now I was into two-timing, three-timing, four-timing, with an endless succession of women.

I suppose that, because I was in a violent world, women thought I would be a violent lover throwing them round the bedroom like Tarzan, having passionate sex up the wardrobes or whatever. If that was their turn-on, they'd have been sadly disappointed. I was always gentle in bed, I cared about the women's emotions, I cared that they got satisfaction, too. I got enough violence at work, I didn't need it in the bedroom. The continual use of body-building steroids, as I've said before, made my sexual appetite insatiable. I lost count of the number of casual encounters I had. At 5ft 9in tall and built like a brick shithouse, I was no film star. It didn't matter a damn.

I once went to visit a mate of mine on the outskirts of Chigwell to discuss a motor I was interested in buying from one of his neighbours. He lived in a classy neighbourhood in a *Birds of a Feather* sort of way; you know, a few dodgy ones here and there among the stockbrokers and ad men, and I was introduced to the neighbour's wife, a nice-looking woman, in her thirties and well turned out in designer gear, a bit of style. Nothing much was said. It didn't need to be. The looks were enough.

I made a point of leaving my phone number in case she or her husband wanted to discuss the car. That was my excuse, anyway.

The next morning, the phone woke me. By midday, we were in bed together.

'That was quick,' I said.

'Yes, when I see something I want, I go for it,' she replied.

A pleasant afternoon ended an hour before her husband

was due back from his City office believing that the little woman had done nothing more interesting with her day than prepare a pasta bake for dinner. I knew this one was too hot. I never went back.

I don't want to spend hours boasting about conquests, but one embarrassing encounter I recall was at the Room at the Top in Ilford. I'd been on the door all evening. We'd had a spot of bother with a couple of hard-cases from Romford. It was settled in our favour but not before one of the likely lads had got a bloodied nose and broken wrist.

The fracas seemed to excite a redhead sitting at the bar. I'd swear I had a glimpse of her knickers at least four times as she crossed her legs seductively. She was waiting at closing time. Usual chat up. 'Can I give you a lift home?'

'Yes, lovely.'

I was switched to supervising the customers leaving in the lift – as the club was over a big store, there was no alternative. The lift arrived. Just me and the redhead were waiting. In we jumped and were straight into a passionate clinch. I knew that a key in the control panel would stop the lift at any floor I liked on the way down. I flicked it. We stopped at seven. She'd unzipped my trousers and was down on her knees. Ahh, seventh heaven. But now I was panicking about other customers I knew would be gathering on the upper floor to get in the lift and make their way home. I could hear people shouting, 'What's going on? Come on, we want to get out.'

So I thought I'd better flick the 'Go' key back on and drop the redhead down at the exit then zoom back up for the punters. But, unfortunately, the urgent pressing of the top-floor button had overridden the down signal and, in an instant, we were back outside the club entrance with the doors sliding back to reveal a blushing doorman hastily doing up his flies and a flustered redhead busily wiping her face with a hanky. There must have been over 100 clubbers there who knew exactly what had gone on.

In gangland, image is all important. Your mistress is often your status symbol, your trophy that shows you're doing the business, making a nice few bob; you've got the four-wheel drive and luxury home conversion in a couple of acres of security fencing in Essex, a few ponies grazing, a pair of Rottweilers and, quite often, an unsuspecting wife happy not to wonder too much about where the bundles of readies for the designer kitchen and Neff oven are coming from. It was like you wanted the best of both worlds. The loyal wife at home with the kids, the piece of totty to impress your underworld cronies.

In my case, there was one simple reason why I never involved my wife or any of my long-term partners in my business activities – they would be far too vulnerable. One sure way for an enemy to hurt you hard would be to go for your wife. If you keep her away from the danger zone, she's not going to be susceptible. If she's up front, part of your business world, she's in danger. If you were on the door at a busy club, she'd be a big distraction because you'd always be looking out for her and not doing your job properly. At home with the kids she's safe. I know it sounds chauvinistic, but it's practical.

So it's the totty, the girls who lap up all the danger and excitement of gangland, who generally get to see the bright lights and the gangsters' get-togethers in dimly lit clubs. That's OK as long as the tail doesn't start wagging the dog. I've seen time and time again how girlfriends start getting their claws in, how they try to influence important decisions, how they try to exercise their own likes and dislikes about different members of a firm.

One girl who was sleeping with a gang boss I know used to go out with one of the underlings in the firm, but they'd fallen out over some jewellery. She'd moved on up the gangland social ladder, so to speak. One night during pillow talk, she said, 'You know that Dave, he told me once he was going to shoot you ...' Whether it was true or not, the cat would be well and truly among the pigeons and poor Dave's future would be looking exceptionally dodgy.

It's amazing the loyalty that some of gangland's women can show and frightening how fickle others can be. I've seen them stick devotedly to some of the most horrible bastards you are ever likely to encounter, yet others seem to make that switch of allegiance at the drop of a hat and for the weirdest of reasons. I've known several who have not only ditched a long-standing boyfriend when he's ended up in nick, they have jumped into bed with the copper who nicked him. I think perhaps there may be a parallel attraction of cops and crooks. They are both involved in danger, intrigue, the thrill of the chase, just operating on different sides of the fence. There is a very fine line between a good policeman and a good crook. They think the same. It's the hunter and the hunted. I think women find both a real turn-on.

A lot of villains live double lives, partly out of choice, partly out of necessity. For most of my adult life, I was splitting myself in two, torn apart trying to be all things to each woman. It's a recipe for disaster at the end of the day. While I was with Denny, I was having a long-standing relationship with Lynn. I was living in two worlds. Denny and the baby were my cornerstone, my sanctuary from all the madness, the violence, the surging drug culture that engulfed my life. When I went home to her, I shut the door and became Mr Normal. The big hunk sitting at the table, being a dad, being a husband, pretending there was no danger out there.

With Lynn, it was different. Lynn was part of my working life. She was streetwise, tough, we were together in the darker side of life where knifings and beatings and drug overdoses were everyday occurrences. Lynn knew how to handle herself in violent and dangerous situations. She was very much part of my security set-up. She was the one who searched the girls for weapons and drugs. And, make no mistake, the female clubbers were more than willing to carry parcels of E or coke into a club, either for themselves, to sell, or to hand over to a boyfriend to serve up. And many weren't averse to carrying a blade down their pants to protect the stash. Lynn walked the walk and she talked the talk. If a big fight suddenly went off in a club, she was there, fearless, composed, brilliant at looking after hysterical women, calming an ugly situation, preventing worse bloodshed and violence.

She also knew when to stand back, she knew when the situation was becoming too fraught for her own safety and it was time, perhaps, to leave quietly through the back door and make for the car while matters were sorted.

When we returned to the flat I'd bought for her, we had a different kind of refuge, a different currency between us, a dependency on each other's strengths and abilities, but nonetheless a beautiful, gentle relationship that was more than a cheating bastard like me deserved.

It was important that I had the Mr Normal image with Denny in Brentwood, even though I'd never pass for the average bank manager. I didn't want people to know what I really did for a living, especially if I'd been involved in a bit of naughtiness. To the neighbours I was just 'in security'. That way, they wouldn't give Denny a bad time, there wouldn't be the nudging and pushing and whispering at the supermarket, 'Oh, she's a villain's wife, you know.'

She was the one who had to take the kids to school, she didn't want to feel uncomfortable every time she stepped out of her own front door. I owed her that. Once a year, we'd take the kids down to our caravan at Clacton and they'd have a lovely six-week holiday on the beach. But I could never stay more than a few days at a time with them. The lure of the nightlife, the excitement of gangland, the adrenalin rush was too much. I was up and down to Clacton throughout the school holidays, one minute cuddly Dad buying ice creams, paddling in the sea; the next, it was back to London, heavy drug scene, club doors to protect, faces to meet, business to discuss.

The influence of gangsters' molls can never be underestimated. I've seen the hardest of men break down and cry over a woman. I've known one man try to kill himself when his mistress said goodbye. The toughest of gangsters are capable of deep emotions and can be destroyed by women.

Equally, women have the capability of inflicting great damage. There never was a truer saying than 'Hell hath no fury like a woman scorned'.

Pillow talk is the most dangerous of all romantic activities and it has betrayed many a villain over the years. A crook is likely to tell a mistress a lot more about his activities than a wife. When the day comes for them to part company, she has confidences to betray that can spell danger to his lifestyle that might even land him in jail. We'd all like to think it would never happen to us, but look at the number of cases where a police prosecution relies on the word of a disgruntled gangster's moll, spilling the beans to get her revenge. They can really fuck you up.

My policy was always to be a bit careful over what I said. If it was serious stuff, the kind of things they didn't need to know about, I'd play it close to my chest. With Denny and Lynn I had two of the most loyal women you could ever wish for. But I still had to play around. Not because I didn't love them – and I did love them equally – but because I was driven by this terrible sexual urge that came from using steroids month after month and I couldn't keep my hands off other women.

I remember several times going to bed with three or four different women within 24 hours and hopefully leaving them all with a smile on their face. I was totally selfish, I wanted more and more sex, I was notching up women like a Wild

West gunfighter. I was like a schoolboy in a sweetshop. And I was helping myself to all the Smarties going.

But that's the way it was. The club scene, the underworld, are male-dominated zones, it's the jungle culture, the lion king syndrome, not just one female in tow, but three, four or five at a time. It could be ferocious at times. You want them all. You want to protect your harem. You see someone moving in on your territory and – Bang! – they're out.

I liked to stop it before it became a problem. If I saw someone making a move on any of my women, I'd walk over and say, 'Do yourself a favour, mate, or you'll get hurt.' That was usually enough. Presence, aura, image was so important in that world, like street actors putting on a show; who's the hardest, who's the most dangerous, whose firm is the biggest? There was something sinister, the ever-present threat of danger hovering over things, that made it like an aphrodisiac cocktail for some women. And many drank deeply.

I was a two-timing bastard and I'm not proud of it, but I can put my hand on my heart and say that I'm still good friends with most of the women who have been important in my life, especially Karen, Denny and Lynn. No grudges there, I hope.

My current girlfriend Kelly is only 24 and I'm 42, so I suppose I could be accused of cradle-snatching. But she's got a wise head on a young body and she has been a fantastic help in sorting my life out. She's knows all my strengths and all my weaknesses and is always there when I need her. She understands my lifestyle and she knows what I have to do. I won't let her down like I've let so many other women down.

I can't believe now how crass I was with my first wife Karen. I was only 17 when we fell in love and got married, a couple of days after walking out of Tottenham Magistrates Court where I'd been up on an ABH charge as a result of soccer hooliganism. I told her, 'Look, love, West Ham is my life. My football and my mates come first and you come second.'

I can't believe I was like that, but that was the reality of the situation then – soccer and soccer violence was more important to me than my wife. I told her, 'Don't ever try to stop me.'

So poor Karen found herself sitting at home all alone from Friday night to Sunday, week in, week out, while I was causing bedlam at football grounds around the country. But she accepted that. I didn't know how well off I was. Karen was a good, straight woman, my first real love, not interested in villainy in any way.

I was working down the dock earning regular money, we had a house and mortgage and then baby Carly came along. I should have been content with that. It's a lot more than many men achieve. But from the moment I started on the club doors, once I got the adrenalin rush, once I discovered how the women flocked round Mr Danger Man, I lost it. From being a football thug with an aimless delight in causing havoc, I was suddenly a superhero in my mind, standing supreme on the doors believing I was God's fucking gift to women. So it went on for most of my years in the muscle game.

The first door job, at Mooros in Stratford, came with built-in violence. The regular doorman, Kieran, a big lump of a rugby player, had been KO'd by a firm from Custom House, which included a semi-pro boxer, and the club were looking for a replacement. And they knew more trouble was brewing. I was a regular in there and one of the security blokes rang me and asked if I would like to work the busy Saturday night stint. I said, 'How much?'

'Forty quid.'

So I reported for duty, not really knowing what to expect, but full of anticipation, ready for anything. Suddenly, there were about 20 geezers at the door and things started getting nasty. But I recognised two of the mob as brothers I'd known for years. It was Dave, a shit-hot fighter, who'd knocked Kieran spark out the previous night. Would I be the next for a right hook now I was there as the new bouncer? They recognised me.

'Hello, Carlton, how you doing?'

'I'm the new doorman.'

Peace broke out. Trouble was avoided. The club were well pleased. And I'd got respect. I was hooked on the buzz of it all. And it wasn't long before the additional perks of the job, in the form of pretty blondes, brunettes and redheads, made me realise this was the life I wanted, not sweating in the bowels of a ship at the Royal Albert Docks.

I'm no great Adonis and my battle scars are evident to see, but the change in the attitude of women once I started door work was nothing short of remarkable. Barmaids, waitresses, dancers and drinkers – whoever – were not just available but gagging for it. Mooros carried a staff of around 15 girls, and they all wanted to be seen leaving with the doorman. An after-hours shag was regarded as a regular everyday bonus. And if I could get three or four door shifts a week at £40 a time, I could make darn sight more than working as a ship's engineer. Three sessions netted me more than I got in seven days in the docks. That was it. I was muscle for hire from then on.

With my new-found status came attitude. You might not realise it, but you get that swagger, that arrogance that sets you apart from the flock. And it's not always a good thing. It makes you a nasty person. It may pull the birds, but it's disastrous for your home life. Karen, Denny, Lynn and many more all found to their cost that they were playing second fiddle to my ego as I strode upwards and onwards into violence and crime.

13

Talking Turkey

My mobile rang before dawn. Nobody, but nobody, rings me then unless it's very, very serious. It took just a few words to snap me awake and let me know that this wasn't just serious, this was perilous. Those few words included heroin, Turks, guns and kidnap. Four members of my firm were in deep, deep, trouble. And it was up to Mr Fixit to sort it before someone got killed.

I want to get it on record straight away that I hate heroin and all it stands for. It's a dirty drug. It carries a stigma. The whole heroin scene is an evil empire and I've never wanted any part of it. My firm knew how I felt and the very word heroin was taboo.

Nevertheless, one of my boys had been lured down that path by talk of a monster cache of smack, worth in excess of £10 million on the streets, being there for the taking in the back office safe of a disused warehouse in East London. Tempting for any villain. It doesn't take much of an imagination to realise that your worldly problems could be over for all time with that sort of cash tucked under the mattress. But given half a brain, it isn't hard to realise that nicking someone's fucking great stash of heroin is likely to bring you the biggest nightmare you'll ever have. And so it proved.

I knew absolutely nothing of what had gone on. But some of my regular boys, people I worked with all the time, people I drank with, were suddenly not around. No phonecalls. No meets for a beer. No calling in for work. I knew from other people that something was going on, something I wouldn't like, something that had to be kept away from me. Then came the dawn phonecall.

'Got to talk to you, Carl.' There was fear in the voice.

We met up a couple of hours later. My mate was on his own but he was speaking for the others.

'We're in deep shit,' he said 'you've got to help us.'

Just how deep soon became clear. The consignment of heroin that had gone missing belonged to a top Turkish gang run by two brothers who dispensed a particularly savage form of underworld justice to anyone who crossed them. The huge parcel of drugs had vanished from its supposedly safe hidey-hole after a gangland tip-off had leaked its whereabouts. This was happening a lot. Villains weren't robbing straight folk any more, they were robbing each other. But robbing from mad Turks with honours degrees in brutality? You've got to be off your head.

MUSCLE

My mate insisted that he wasn't responsible and neither were the other boys. They were fingered because a geezer we did a lot of minding work for, between the UK and Amsterdam and various other places, was the Turks' main suspect. If he'd nicked it, or had been behind it, then my boys had to be involved. That's how the Turks were looking at it. My firm was in the frame. And my mates hadn't breathed a word to me for two weeks because they knew how much I despised the whole heroin scene.

In that fortnight, three of the boys had been held prisoner and had had guns thrust into their mouths as the heavy-duty Turks tried to frighten confessions out of them and get their stash back, or the £10 million it was worth. This was obviously the top level of this filthy trade and these guys were going to stop at nothing until they found their gear. I needed to know how my people were involved. You don't get all this shit flying about without good reason.

They were evasive. It was all a mistake, they said. I needed to put myself about to find some answers. Someone had to be in deep to merit the attention of a room full of angry Turks shoving machine-guns and pistols in their mouths.

I found out from different sources that the smack had gone missing while it was supposedly being guarded by a couple of brothers we knew. They were pals of this other fella, who was the main suspect in the eyes of the Turks, who I'll call M to protect him and us. I dug and dug around but nobody knew the full story, and you wouldn't expect them to in such a volatile situation. I was confused myself. I felt sure my boys wouldn't be involved. These were friends and we'd talked about it and we'd all said we wouldn't dirty our hands with heroin. My instinct was to give them the benefit of the doubt and hope the Turkish Mafia would do the same.

No such luck. Soon the rumours were buzzing. So and so is going to get killed. So and so is going to get his brains blown out if he doesn't turn up for a meeting. Everyone was pointing the finger at everyone else. It was mayhem, dangerous, dangerous mayhem. Gangsters were coming down to London from up North sniffing around.

When we met for a drink at a mate's club, there were faces about we hadn't seen before. Menacing faces, most of them bearing distinctly Turkish features and ominous bulges under their long coats. People were here, people were there, conversations were being whispered, people were being watched. I turned to my mate and said, 'Right, I need to know what the fuck is going on. You're not telling me the truth. This is getting too heavy and we need to sort it.'

He said, 'OK, Carl, I'll tell you what I know.'

In short, the boys believed M had had the smack away and sold it. Because they were associates of M, the Turks thought they must know the answers.

'But we don't, Carl, honest. We haven't touched the gear,' he bleated.

I couldn't swallow their story. I pointed out that M was still around and if anyone had just had a £10 million hit with a parcel of heroin, even if they'd sold it at half price, they'd be on their way to Copacabana Beach by now, not hanging around Hoxton. Your first priority would be to get as far away as humanly possible from a very nasty firm of irate Turks. I knew M well, I'd worked with him, I liked him, I trusted him. I couldn't believe he'd be that dumb.

I rang him. 'Get round to mine tomorrow, we need to talk.'

He was there first thing in the morning.

'Look,' I said, 'I don't want any lies. Look me in the eyes and tell me you didn't nick that heroin and haven't been involved in getting rid of it for anyone else.'

His eyes fixed mine with a kind of intensity that satisfied me that whatever he said next would be the truth.

'I swear on my children's lives I'm not involved. You've got to believe me, I'm begging you. Everyone is turning against me. You are the only one who can help me.'

His eyes, now so close to tears, convinced me that he was indeed the victim of a dangerous and wrongful allegation that stood to cost him dearly. He was in bits. He repeated what I'd already said to the other boys. 'If I'd had 10 million away, would I be sitting here?'

He convinced me. But the world out there was still seething with rumours that he was the big shot who'd had the drugs away and it was only a matter of time before the Turks turned up the heat. The word on the street was that somebody was going to get kidnapped or tortured, unless the Turks got satisfaction.

A couple of other mates, living in Colchester, were also convinced that M was innocent and offered him and his family protection at their homes, away from the possibility of kidnap. The Turks had done their homework and they knew where everybody lived. We were dealing with the premier league here.

I wanted to know why I hadn't been alerted earlier, why the situation had been allowed to run out of control. My mate said, 'Be real, Carlton, we know what you're like. You'd have said bollocks and gone steaming in and we'd have a gang war on our hands. We thought we could sort it our way but now we know it's down to you.'

I reckoned a lot of it was a load of cock and bull and the real reason was that they knew I'd go apeshit because heroin was involved.

There was a 24-hour ultimatum given by the Turkish mob. If the matter wasn't settled, they'd want M and his family handed over. We met them and said, 'No way.' The bastards then said it wouldn't make any difference because they knew where brothers, sisters, cousins, even grandmas, lived and, if the matter wasn't wrapped up soon, if M didn't come forward, the relatives would be dead. You knew these guys weren't to be fucked with. The pressure was intense.

The Turks' gang boss, the mastermind behind the whole heroin importation, had even flown to England personally to try to nail the thief who'd nicked his stash. He didn't speak a word of English and the negotiations were conducted through an interpreter. It didn't make them any the less menacing. These were grade A gangsters. And we were talking life and death here.

There were four people the Turks believed stood between them and the recovery of their £10 million. And they wanted to take them all to an empty warehouse over at Barking and interrogate them under a truth drug. I could hardly believe my ears. One thing is for sure, I thought, if the boys leave the club and go to the warehouse, they probably won't ever be back again. I expressed my fears.

No, said the Turks, we won't harm them, we just want to question them under a truth serum.

I didn't like it one bit. I reckoned they were likely to get well and truly kebabbed, the mood the Turks were in. I suggested, as a compromise, that we, the London firm, should do the interrogation in front of everybody. This was heavy shit and I felt I needed to step in to stop someone getting hurt real bad. These idiots around me had got right out of their league. They were good muscle, good at what we did, but now it was the international league giving them grief whether they deserved it or not.

To my surprise, the Turks agreed to me grilling the London boys under the truth drug and I drove to the warehouse in Barking a few hours beforehand to check it out to make sure there wasn't any funny business going on. First, I got myself a shooter. I knew I wasn't going out on this one without protection. I stomped into an empty back office that looked like a stage set for a KGB torture movie. There was an old desk, a couple of old cupboards, a lightbulb overhead. It was cold, dank and sinister. I spotted a towel holder, the roller type favoured by big companies, and slipped the gun behind it. It was a couple of yards away. I did a couple of practice dives at it to make sure I could grab the gun in a matter of seconds if things turned nasty.

The four boys arrived later. They were shitting themselves. I said, 'Look, I believe you, but it's not me you've got to convince.'

The Turks pulled up outside in two limos and three of them walked in, stony-faced, malevolent. The other two stayed in the motors as look-outs. We'd agreed three on each side, no more. The Turkish brothers, now moody and scowling, came into the back office and started pulling open the cupboard doors and generally checking all round. They looked through the desk drawers, through some old cardboard boxes. Nothing. They were confident there were no traps, no surprises, waiting for them. My heart was pumping by now. They'd passed the roller towel several times. They'd looked at it. But they didn't check behind it. If they'd found the gun, it could have blown the whole thing. There's no way they wouldn't have thought it hadn't been planted with the deliberate intention of killing them.

I said, 'Right, I'll do all the talking. I'll question them and you listen. You can say what you want to say afterwards. OK?' There were nods of agreement all round.

The Turks had somehow acquired the truth drug – at least they said the powder was a truth drug – from a chemist's. I didn't know you could buy it over the counter but we had to accept their word. The four lads took the drug, and swilled it down with water like they'd got nothing to hide. They obviously wanted to get the ordeal over and done with as quickly as possible. A couple of them were sweating even though it was a cold night. I was feeling edgy myself. It was all a bit unreal.

The Turks insisted that the 'suspects' were tied to the chairs in case they tried to make a break for it. Not tight bonds, just ropes that weren't causing them any pain, just enough to restrain them. We all waited for the effects of the truth drug to take hold. Five minutes, six minutes, ten minutes. The tension was making everyone jittery. The Turkish brothers were becoming more jumpy, their eyes set firmly on the prisoners roped in their chairs, waiting for a reaction.

'Are you sure this will work?' I asked.

Yeah, yeah, it's been used before, said the Turks.

With that, the eyes of the boys glazed over. They were in the grip of the serum. I stood in front of them.

'You all know who I am,' I said. 'I'm going to ask you some questions.' I put the key question to them straight away, one by one. 'Do you know anything about the gear that's gone missing?'

'No.'

'No.'

'No.'

'No.' One of them added, 'I swear on my life, Carlton, I never had it.'

I asked them if they knew where the heroin was being stashed.

No again.

I asked them if they knew who might have taken it.

No.

The Turks interrupted me and asked me to put a series of other questions to them. I can't remember the exact details now, but they wanted to crack the London lads. My main concern was that the Turkish drug barons were becoming more and more agitated as the questioning went on. They weren't going to be happy with anything but a full sobbing confession. But if the boys hadn't done it, they weren't about to confess.

I told the Turks, 'Look, it's your truth drug, you've got to accept their answers.'

With that, one of the boys lurched forward and started puking all over his trousers. Then he fell off the chair, kicking out on the floor.

Two of them started crying. 'Please, please, we swear on our babies' lives ...' They were terrified, shivering, they thought they were about to die. It was pitiful to watch.

I was certain by now that they hadn't had the heroin but there was no convincing those mad bastard Turks.

'We get the truth,' one of them hissed, 'we get your wives and your daughters and we fuck them in front of you. Then we chop them up.'

I couldn't believe the venomous filth pouring out of their mouths. I was ready to blow. I could feel the anger and loathing boiling up inside. I thought, I've got a gun. I'm going to do these cunts. They've gone too far.

Whatever their rules in their own country, they'd pushed it too far now. All four of the prisoners were in the full throes of the truth drug now. This was supposed to be an interrogation conducted in cool and controlled conditions. It had become mental torture. The fear and the tension had brought all four of them to the point of collapse, big lumps of men had become quaking wrecks.

I moved a couple of paces to where the shooter was hidden, cocked and ready for action. At the last second, I thought, No, no, we're going to have a bloodbath if I grab the shooter. I was sure they were armed. All I wanted to do was get the fellas off the hook and out of this nightmare as quickly as possible. A gunfight wouldn't help.

The Turks made it clear they were still far from happy with the denials but agreed to release them all. We drove back to my pal's club mightily relieved for the time being, but still apprehensive about the threats hanging over the four boys.

M and his family continued to suffer through a barrage of rumours and accusations. I was certain his name had been stuck up as a scapegoat and someone, somewhere, was playing a dangerous game of hide the heroin. But who? All the Turks had to go on was guilt by association, that's all. The trouble was, that's all they needed. People were falling out over it, trust among the firm had vanished, harsh words and threats were everyday occurrences. I kept wondering myself if I was wrong about the boys and they really had gone for the big time and nicked the smack and now were out of their depth. If you are playing with the big boys, you've got to act like big boys, operate on their level. My favourite saying – 'If you talk the talk, you've got to walk the walk' – was never more apt. No, surely, I thought, they are not capable of it. I prayed I was right.

We'd done a bit of naughty stuff for people over the years, not heavy organised crime, but some decent earners and we'd been pretty successful. Now this was a different league altogether. I knew for sure that I'd never touch the stuff with a mile-long barge pole. Inwardly, I was sure my boys wouldn't either. Or would they?

Something had to give to break up this cloud of suspicion hanging over us, and in particular over M. The Turks were insisting he was the prime suspect. They demanded that we hand over M at midnight, at the end of the 24-hour ultimatum, so they could carry out their own brand of interrogation and retribution. I'd seen what they were capable of. I said, 'No way.' And I immediately arranged for M and his family to move into my house in Brentwood where they could get round-the-clock protection. We were driving back from Colchester on the motorway when my mobile rang. It was the Turks.

'We want your friend. You must hand him over immediately.'

I snapped back, 'I'm not handing him over to you or anybody.'

He shouted, 'We have an agreement ...'

I told him there was no agreement. I'd done the truth drug questioning and I'd done my best to try to sort matters out, but I'd never agreed to hand M over to the Turks.

'You are fucking us about,' said one of the brothers.

I was getting angry. 'Who the fucking hell are you talking to?' I said. 'Go fuck yourself. Keep on like that and I'll come and give you some.'

M was white and trembling. He knew this was trouble that wasn't going away.

Now we had two families packed into my home. Two wives, kids everywhere, and I decided the only sensible precaution I could take was to sit up all night, suitably tooled up, to make sure no crazy bastards came through that door and started hurting people.

The phone rang close to midnight. It was my mate from the club, shitting himself.

'Where is he?' he asked. 'They want him back. The deadline is up.'

I said, 'Hold on, it's not my fucking deadline. What the fuck is going on? I was only brought into this at the last minute and I still don't know the truth. Why was I kept out of the picture? Who's hiding something they don't want me to know about. Until I get some answers, M is staying exactly where he is.'

He muttered, 'You've got to turn him in ... they want him bad.'

I asked my mate if the Turks were still at the club. He said they were.

'Right,' I said, 'I'm coming over to do the pair of cunts. I'm going to come and give it to them. The club's closed, isn't it? I'm getting in my motor now.'

He panicked, 'No, no, we don't want any trouble at the club. I knew you'd be like this.'

I told him I thought the Turks were pushing their luck too far. 'I can't handle all this shit about hurting wives and children,' I said. 'Tell the Turks to go fuck themselves.' I slammed the phone down in fury. Then I turned to M and said, 'Right, you've got to get yourself out of here at first light and make a run for it. Have you got a gun?'

He had.

I told him, 'Just disappear. I don't even want to know where you are.'

He shot off out in the morning after we'd checked the

coast was clear and headed for a safe house. His wife was left sobbing on my doorstep. She was in pieces. She was terrified she'd never see him alive again. I felt gutted for the whole family. I knew I had to get to the bottom of the matter for their sakes, for all our sakes.

The next thing I knew, M had been kidnapped, as had a couple of the other lads. I reckon someone gave up the address of the safe house to save their own skin. That's the only conclusion I could come to. How else could they have found him?

Now the situation was desperate. The Turks had stopped even pretending to be reasonable. They'd got M and the others held prisoner in a block of flats and they had started to torture them. No truth serum now, just brutal, vicious systematic torture. They were all stripped bollock naked, tied to chairs once again, this time with skin cutting wire, and burned with lit cigarettes on their arms, legs and bodies. Then they had electric cattle prods jabbed into their bollocks, reminiscent of the descriptions I remembered reading about the Richardson torture gang in South London in the Fifties.

M was subjected to a dagger being thrust right through his leg and out the other side. For three days the victims – for that is certainly what they had become by now – were beaten, humiliated, starved and hurt as the Turks tried to extract the truth, or what they believed was the truth, out of them by brute force.

If I'd been with them, I know I couldn't have handled it without going apeshit. I'd been involved in the muscle game most of my life, a hard old game, but what these boys went through at the hands of those bastards was a different dimension. They would only let them go when they came to the conclusion that they must be innocent because no one would suffer that degree of punishment for three days if they could escape by making a confession. They could only say, 'We don't know anything about the smack,' so many times. Finally, the Turks freed them.

When I saw M a couple of days afterwards, he dropped his trousers and said, 'Look what they've done, Carl.' His body was scarred top to bottom with knife injuries, cigarette burns and electric shock wounds. He was traumatised. He was as pale as a ghost. You could see the fear still in his eyes. All of them were traumatised, one so badly that he later committed suicide. They'd come face to face with the type of ruthlessness that the international drugs rackets have spawned over the last 20 years. A barbaric régime to defend their corner in the deadly trade of heroin dealing. Bad enough on the face of it but, realistically, I suppose, they were lucky to be alive. These kind of guys kill for a lot less than ten million.

I was certain beyond doubt by now – 1,000 per cent certain – that M had not been involved. He was still living with the nightmare and would continue to do so until the real truth came out. It did, eventually, but by then four lives, even more, had been damaged beyond repair. It seems that the wife of one of the boys who'd been tortured was a slag with a serious cocaine problem ... and had a habit of sleeping around. One of her lovers was a small-time North London crook whose name would feature large in my future. Right now, he was the missing link in the heroin scam. He'd picked up during pillow talk as he was rumping the slag that her old man was minding a £10 million stash of smack. She showed him the warehouse where it was being kept and even managed to get him a duplicate set of keys. He got in there with some mates and had the lot away. A tart's betrayal had brought all this shit on us.

I was just happy we'd got to the bottom of the matter at long last and the shadow of suspicion was no longer hanging over M. He told me, 'Carlton, you are the only one who stood by me. I honestly thought I was a goner.' I was just pleased for his kids. In the time they were staying at my house, I'd seen their confused faces wondering where Daddy was and why they couldn't go out to play with the other children.

To this day I don't know whether the missing heroin was ever recovered, or whether the Turks got their ten million, and I don't care. All I was grateful for was the war was now being fought on someone else's turf, not ours.

★　　　★　　　★

The next time I was to encounter the name of the north London crook was after the murders of Tony Tucker and the others at Rettendon. The investigation had almost ground to a halt when a member of the murder gang was persuaded by an undercover cop to turn squealer and shop the others. He admitted he had driven the getaway motor on the night of the killings. In exchange for a new identity, he put up the names of Micky Steele and Jack Whomes as the men whose trigger-fingers ended the lives of my pals that cold December night.

During his time assisting the police and giving evidence at Steele and Whomes's trial, he was known simply as Bloggs 19. Under the Witness Protection Scheme, all prisoners involved as witnesses or supergrasses in major crimes are given a Bloggs codename by prison staff so that their real identity remains a secret. He has now vanished off the face of the earth; every record of his existence has been erased, and I can only say good riddance. His whole involvement in the case stinks and there are a lot of people out there still believing the wrong men are in jail for the murders.

The whole business with the Turks was about money. Of course it was. That's why we are villains and don't hold down a nine-to-five job for a living. But the amount of money washing around, most of it from the drugs trade, is becoming unbelievable. I've had £2 million cash to mind for someone. Moving it about is where the risk is. Robbers are robbing other robbers more than ever these days. So the people with the money employ muscle like me to move it for them, no questions asked. It was all routine work on top of earning from the club doors and other bits and pieces.

One night, I collected a cardboard video box from a client, ready to move it the next day to another address, and took it to my home. I had a quick look inside. Banknotes, hundreds of notes. At a guess, probably £250,000. A quarter of a million. But I had to get off to work on a club door. So I shoved the box in the bedroom cupboard and said goodnight to Denny. When I got back in the early hours the following morning, she was still awake, trembling.

I said, 'What's up, luv?'

She said, 'You've got all that fucking money in that box and just left it in the cupboard. If someone knew it was there and had come after it, what the fuck do you think would have happened to me and the girls?'

She hadn't slept a wink. She was livid. And rightly so. It hit me there and then like a ton of bricks. I was acting stupid. I was letting my family down. Of course, I should never have left them in the house with all that cash. It was a lesson learned and it never happened again.

I sometimes knew whose money I was shifting and where it was coming from. But if they chose not to tell me, I didn't ask questions. I didn't want to know. I was just Mr Deliveryman. I had a reputation as a safe pair of hands and it was well-paid work. I've sat in a room with people counting out £1 million in used notes and walked out with a parcel like I was picking up a take-away pizza.

Denny's scare made me realise how careless I was getting. She said, 'How do you know you are not being followed on any one of those jobs? For that kind of money you are a dead man. A dead husband and a dead father.'

She was right again.

Then one day, along came the men from Bogota. They'd heard that I was the man who could help with the distribution of their goods in Britain. For goods, read cocaine, the boom drug in Britain, turning over millions a day for the suppliers. They'd heard about my reputation and wanted to talk business. I met them in a hotel in London.

We talked big money. Million and millions. I know they weren't talking bullshit. I'd seen with my own eyes the demand for Charlie round the club scene. I could have said, 'Yes, let's go for the big time.' But that warning voice inside was telling me to be careful. These were big players again. They weren't the sort of people you could mess around with and say, 'Well, I'll do it for a while, then I'll pack it all in when I'm rich.' These people don't let you go. You sell your soul to the men from Colombia.

Some of my boys were keen to get involved. I said, 'No, this is not our game.' Even though we had spent £30,000 of our own money setting up a moody company to smuggle in hundreds of kilos of coke, I knew this was dangerous territory, too damned dangerous. The Colombians were pushing for a deal. They organised a big consignment of Charlie to be smuggled into another country and we were due to go out to pick it up for distribution on the London scene. But the vibes were all wrong. I didn't like it one tiny bit, even given the thought of the big bucks at the end of it. I pulled the plug. And to this day I reckon it was the best £30,000 I've ever lost. I'm in control of my life, not murky taskmasters 5,000 miles away. I'm a street boy from East Ham not an international drug-dealer. And I can sleep easy on my pillow at night. Just.

14

Welcome Home, Son

For 25 years, I was tortured by the memory of the son I gave away. Not a birthday went by when I didn't shed a few tears wondering what had happened to him. Was his life a happy one? Did he know he was adopted? Did he look like me? Would he ever come looking for me? All I'd got were just a few faded photographs of a bonny little boy, a few weeks old, to remind me of the day my life was turned upside-down.

My teenage sweetheart and her parents had thought it best that he must be put up for adoption. We were kids who'd made a mistake, so our wishes were unimportant. The agonies of parting with him had seared an angry memory in my mind that never faded. I was wracked by guilt thinking that I should have fought harder to keep him.

Every April, I had a private celebration of another year of his life; milestones like 18 and 21 were particularly emotional. My boy had reached manhood and these were moments we should be sharing. I waited, hoped, prayed there would be a knock on the door. Nothing. Year after year after year. Nothing.

I'd look at many a young man in the street and think, Could that be my son? Every Christmas, I felt that there was this huge gap in my life, a void – something, someone, was missing and things were never going to be right until we found each other.

Should I go looking for him? No, the pain of rejection if he didn't want to see me would be too much to bear. Sounds silly, in my line of work, to be so emotional about someone who was just a distant memory. But that's the way it was.

I never, ever, gave up hope that he'd come looking for me one day. I felt that there was a sort of telepathy in the air that would draw him to me. But as the years flew by it seemed little more than a daydream.

Then one day I got a call on my mobile as I was out at the shops in Romford buying a new tracksuit. It was Denny.

'Are you sitting down?' she asked.

That usually means bad news, a death even, and I thought about Mum and Dad.

Denny went on, 'Your son has turned up.'

Butterflies surged up in my stomach. All I could say was, 'Nah, nah.' I thought for a second she was winding me up. But, no, Denny knew how I felt about my long-lost son. She knew what it meant. She knew how much I wanted him to walk through the door. We'd talked about it often enough. I'd joked with her, 'Supposing he's a Millwall supporter?'

Denny wouldn't be cruel. So this had to be true.

'His mate is here, do you want a word with him?.'

Did I want a word? Is the Pope a Catholic? 'Put him on the phone.'

'Hello, Mr Leach. You've got a son, Matty, and I'm his best mate, Gary. He wants to meet you.'

The name was different. When he went off to his new home and uncertain future back in 1976, he was called Carlton James on his birth certificate. I said, 'What's his date of birth?' It was spot on. I asked a few more questions to establish that this wasn't some terrible mistake that was going to leave me despondent again. It all added up. This was my long-lost boy, and he'd come to find me. I was dumbstruck, which was something else for a man with a reputation for talking the hind leg off a donkey.

I can hardly remember driving the ten miles back home to Brentwood. It was the weirdest feeling. What should I do? How do you play a situation like this? I'd waited 25 years for this moment and now I didn't know what to say, what to do. But you can't put a script to an emotional drama like this. Let it happen naturally, I decided.

I pulled up outside my house full of anticipation. Out came a fucking great bloke, head shaved, earrings, covered in tattoos and at least 6ft 7in tall. He looked like Lurch from TV. I looked him up and down and said, 'I hope you're not my fucking son!' I was laughing because it really wouldn't have mattered.

He grinned. 'No,' he said, 'your son is indoors.'

'Thank fuck for that,' I said. I walked through the door and Matty was standing there. It didn't matter about words. We just hugged each other and cried. I couldn't believe my dream had come true after all this time. We cried some more and we talked all day. Denny was in tears, too, caught up in the emotion of our tearful reunion.

I wanted to know everything about the missing years. I rang my mum and dad, I rang Carly, I rang everybody who needed to know.

'My boy is back.'

It was a power-packed heart-tugging emotion, the most wonderful day of my life. After all the terrible things that had happened over the last few years, suddenly something good had come in through the door with the year 2001.

It was soon like we had never been apart. We bonded instantly, father and son, and talked into the night. He said he had not tried to contact his mother. He didn't want to have anything to do with her parents either.

'I know you wouldn't have done it if you hadn't been forced,' he said. He'd studied all the paperwork in the case – or as much as he was allowed to see – and he knew the truth. It had taken him more than two years to track me down, plus several three-hour sessions of counselling to prepare him for the day we were finally reunited.

He would have found me earlier, he said, but the vital piece of the jigsaw that was missing, as in all adoption cases, was my surname. He knew my Christian name was Carlton, but until he discovered that my surname was Leach, he knew there was little chance of tracing me with the scant details at his disposal. He'd been to a number of old addresses but it was always the same 'Sorry, he's moved on. New address not known.' Then he picked up the fact that I was probably living in the Brentwood area of Essex. He and a mate sat down with the electoral roll for the town and systematically worked through it street by street until they arrived at the name Leach, Carlton Norman.

Matty told me that even when he was certain he had found the right address, he pulled up outside with his mate Gary and suddenly lost his nerve. After all the painstaking weeks and months of looking for his missing dad, his bottle went.

'I couldn't get out of the car,' he said. 'I was rooted to the seat. If Gary hadn't been with me and made me knock, I would have turned the car around and driven off.'

Matty, it transpired, had been adopted by a great couple and was living in one of the nicest parts of the South-East, Little Chalfont, in the prosperous commuter belt of Berkshire. It was a far cry from the grim streets of East London where he'd been born 25 years earlier. He'd known from a boy that he was adopted although his new mum and dad knew little about me or his mother. He never told them that he was looking for me in case it upset them. But once his mission was complete, he broke the news to them and they were delighted.

The surprises weren't over yet. When I visited him for the first time at the home in Little Chalfont he now shared with his wife, I was amazed to see how many of the same videos as mine were on his shelves – *Terminator, Rocky, Mad Max* – all the bruiser movies I loved. He was into bodybuilding like me, had tattoos like me and earned a living from muscle like me, though in his case it was building up the muscles of fitness fanatics as manager of a gym in Slough. He called me into his bedroom.

'Look at this, Dad.'

I could hardly believe it. His reading material was exactly the same – the biography of renowned gangland heavy Dave Courtney; the Essex Boys book by Bernard O'Mahoney which had been made into a hit film and featured the deaths of my friends at Rettendon – so many of the same books I had read. It was freaky. My boy was like a clone of his dad. Good or bad, I don't know, but it wasn't going to take a DNA test to confirm this chip off the old block. For me, it was the happy ending I had yearned for. If I die tomorrow, I'll go happy in the knowledge that my son came back.

A little memento of the day he found me, a lighter with 'Dad' engraved on it and dated February 2001, will always be among my most treasured possessions.

But with the happiness of our reunion came problems I found hard to handle. Of course, he wanted to know everything about me. He knew I'd been around the muscle game for many years and had done club doors and security, but there were grey areas of my life I wasn't prepared to share. I wasn't a normal dad. I wasn't a bank manager or a computer salesman. I'd done things, been places, met people, that no normal Dad would ever do. I'd hurt people for money. I'd been around the drugs boom. People had died. How much do

I tell Matty? I don't ever want him to regret the day he found me. I needed to be careful. Do I say 'Look, I've been a bit of a villain, son, but you know how things are out in that tough old world.' I didn't like it. I didn't want to be apologising for what I was, even though some aspects were pretty unsavoury. In the end, I decided to sit down with him and watch a video of the Channel Five programme I'd made with Kate Kray for the *Hard Bastards* TV series. It proved to be very traumatic, very difficult for him to understand. The film portrayed me as some savage gangland thug caught up in a terrible triple murder. Trying to explain 'Yes, son, this was my world but at the same time I am a loving and caring father who wants rid of his past,' was one of the hardest things I've ever had to do. I took it a step at a time. I didn't need him believing that this was a glamorous world his dad was in and him wanting to follow in my footsteps. I know the dangers in that all too well.

I think he understood where I was coming from. Then when he'd be out socialising in pubs and clubs, people would start saying things like, 'I know your dad,' and wanting to be around him because of me and my reputation and I started worrying. I knew the pattern, I knew the route it could lead him down. But happily he's got his head screwed on and, while we've got many common interests, he's content to be a straight guy earning an honest living. Finding Matty, or Matty finding me, was a richness money can't buy. Whatever I've been, this was a story with a joyful ending that anyone can relate to, gangster or greengrocer.

I haven't met his adoptive parents yet, but I gather they are pretty cool about the situation. They've done a great job raising him and his adopted sister. I will meet them one day and I will thank them personally. I know he's my flesh and blood, but he's their son. He's got genes that make him what he is, the same genes that make me what I am. I'm glad he's had a good life. It's just a shame he supports Tottenham — it's worse than Millwall! My worst fear. We've had a good laugh about it and he's even promised to send me a Tottenham calendar. I told him not to bother, I'll rip it up. It's all good-natured stuff. I know I'll convert him to West Ham one day. He wants me to go to watch Tottenham with him. I've told him if he bought me 20 tickets I wouldn't set foot in White Hart Lane.

He really gels with my eldest daughter Carly; they mess about and wind each other up. He gets on great with my other kids as well. I suppose the greatest bonus for me was not only finding my son, but learning for the first time that I was also a grandad. He's got a lovely little girl, a real charmer. She was 14 months old when I first saw her and I just melted ... blonde hair, blue eyes, a real stunner. Her name is Angel and she looks like an angel. I just wish I could see a lot more of her.

Unfortunately, since me and Matty met up, his marriage has hit trouble and I just hope I'm not to blame. It's a lot for a wife to take on board, finding out that your long-lost father-in-law is a well-known hard-case from the East End with some very dubious connections.

I'm trying to walk away from the bad things in my life but it's very hard. You are what you are. You've chosen your destiny, or destiny has chosen you, and you have to be man enough to face the consequences. The Devil will always demand his pound of flesh. You can't turn the clock back and say, 'I'm sorry I did this,' or 'I'm sorry I did that,' because it was my choice to lead my lifestyle, nobody forced me to. If someone asked me what would I do differently, and what would I change, I couldn't answer them. I don't know. How do you know it's a mistake until you make it. It probably seemed the right thing at the time. You've got to live with your mistakes. That's the way it goes. You've got to hope that some of those mistakes help make you a stronger person for the future.

One decision I know was right was turning down invitations by my old pal Vicky Dark who was around when Matty was born and put up for adoption. He asked me to join his gang of bank robbers. It was almost an honour in the East End to be considered tough enough for armed robberies. I idolised him and I was tempted.

He was a year or two older than me and he could really look after himself – great fighter, karate expert, he had that aura about him that set him apart from the crowd. A lot of people said he was just plain bad. He wasn't. He taught me to have bottle when the odds were against us.

One night in a West End club, we went for a piss together and found ourselves in the toilet with about 12 Chelsea fans looking for bother. One of them asked me, 'You West Ham, mate?'

Knowing we were seriously outnumbered, I said, 'No, mate, what you on about?' I thought duck and run would be best.

Vic got his back to the wall, turned to one of them and went – Bang! The geezer was on the deck. Then he went – Bang! Whack! Bang! – and they were falling like fucking ninepins. I joined in. Wallop! Another on the floor with a bleeding nose. With Vic you thought you could never be beaten. We took the lot out. He taught me the value of loyalty, trust and confidence in your mates that stayed with me for ever.

I drew the line, though, when we were driving home one night after a bit of a barny in the bar of the old Hackney dog track and he said, 'Carl, fancy doing a few robberies? I've got a shooter. I reckon you'd be great at it.'

It was a time when bank and building society robberies were still common, 'pavement work' we called it, and I did fancy the money. But I said, 'No, not my scene Vic.'

About seven or eight of them were at it. They did three or four banks, two or three post offices, all in the space of a few weeks. They were raking it in and spending like there was no tomorrow. It was inevitable they were going to get nicked.

I spent the next nine-and-a-half years visiting Vic in prison. He said, 'You made the right call not joining the gang, Carlton. You don't want to be in here.'

I've never done bird – although it's been a pretty close shave at times – and the reason was Vicky Dark. Vic got trapped on that vicious roundabout – you do bird and when you come out you can't get work. No one wants to know you. So you turn to crime again. Only 11 months after getting parole, he carried out an armed robbery on the Penthouse Club, where I used to work, and ended up getting a 15-year stretch. So he's done 23 years inside when his life was worth so much more, half his life banged up. I hope he can make it back but, like so many long-term prisoners, he became institutionalised and found life hard when he walked out through those gates. I would have liked to be there for him, like he was there for me so many times. Thanks to him I don't ever need to tell Matty that I'm an ex-con.

I was happy to tell Matty about a true diamond in my security firm who I'd trust with my life, a guy called Gary Hunter, a former Royal Marine we nicknamed Fearless. There was never a truer name. He was muscle with style, hard as nails but a man with wit and charisma who could keep you fascinated for hours with stories of his exploits. He was just so interesting. Nothing frightened Gary. Fear was not in his vocabulary. He could do anything, he absolutely amazed me.

He had spent years as an army instructor, was a master at Thai boxing and held all sorts of martial arts qualifications. He was as fit and tough as it was possible to be, with lightning reactions; slim, wiry and muscular, like a striking cobra. And because of his military background, he knew how to obey orders. You couldn't have a better pair of eyes watching your back. We had a great working rapport and could virtually read each other's minds without a word being spoken.

The first time we went water-skiing together down at Point Clear near Clacton – a bit of a villain's playground in the Eighties and Nineties, I remember him starting off on two skis behind the speedboat, then ditching one and going solo, then putting the tow rope triangle round his neck at 45mph. One slip and he would have died from a broken neck. To crown it all, at the end he pulled alongside the quay and flipped out, landing perfectly on the side with a big grin on his face. That was Gary, always taking it to the edge. Not flash. He did it because he could.

We once stopped outside his house in Colchester to pick up his wife to go out for dinner and Fearless put his hands on a lamp-post outside, his feet on the wall of his house and ran right up it, about 20ft, and called to his missus through the window, 'Hurry up, we're waiting.' He was like a fucking monkey at climbing.

On one debt job, we went to collect £50,000 owed to a mate with a car firm in Woodford. We strolled into the geezer's office, a big sort he was, and I pretended I was the garage owner's brother just flown back from Tenerife to help pick up the debt. I was holding my hand inside my coat like I'd got a gun. I leaned over him and said 'I want that fucking dough. I'll give you ten minutes and I'll be back. Get it sorted.'

He moaned and groaned about it and said he couldn't raise the cash in that time. As I turned away, I whacked him with a backhand right across his face. It sent him spinning round in his swivel chair. Quick as lightning, Gary had hit him – Crack! – as he spun back towards me like a ping-pong ball, I belted him again and said, 'Right, that's your warning. If you haven't got the money in ten minutes we'll finish the game. Then we'll put you through the glass doors and your missus can pick up the pieces.'

It looked like the whole thing was rehearsed. It wasn't. Fearless was one of those people who can read a situation quick as lightning and react as fast. Not surprisingly, the bloke started to cough up the 50 grand in instalments. Then he stopped. So I went looking for him up in North London. This time I trapped him in his Porsche and whacked him with a powerful 4,000 volt stun-gun. He shit himself. His hair stood right up on end from the electric shock. I said, 'Right, cunt, next time it's serious. This is personal now, you're taking the piss.' He never missed another instalment.

I felt this was an area of my life I could justify to Matty. In my world, this was legit business. We were filling a vacuum in the system where the due process of law would be a waste of time. With debts like these, you can spend thousands of pounds on lawyers, you can get court judgments, but you still can't get your money. A visit from CN Leach Esq, debt-collector, usually succeeds where any amount of litigation will fail. If people came to us first, if they didn't piss about for two years with lawyers and courts, they'd get their money a whole lot quicker and save themselves at least £5,000 in legal fees. We're a necessary evil in a corrupt world. We may slap a few people about a bit from time to time, but how else do you deal with piss-taking scum who don't pay their debts?

I think Matty respects what we do. I had to point out to him that while the success of any outfit like ours depends on reputation – the more fearsome, the better – the downside is that your reputation can precede you and cause unwanted problems when you least need them.

One such example occurred one Bank Holiday when a team of us went to down to Hastings, with wives and girlfriends, for a bit of relaxation, a few drinks, a nice meal, ice cream on the front, that sort of thing.

We strolled into a club in the evening that we'd been to before, us big lumps from up the smoke and their molls, plus a local 'face' known as Nick from Hastings. What I hadn't realised was the fact that, since our previous visit, word had reached the club manager, Johnny, that my firm was running out of control in London and if we came through the door it meant serious aggro for anyone who got in our way. As we strolled in the panicky manager called me into the back office.

'Look, I don't want any trouble. I run a respectable club here ...' etc.

For 20 minutes, me and Nick persuaded him that we were just a group of blokes out for an enjoyable day with our women and the last thing we wanted was any aggravation. We were at the seaside to get away from bother, not to cause it. He was finally soothed.

'OK,' he said, 'but the licensing people will close me down if I've got trouble here.'

I told him, 'Johnny, mate, don't you worry about a thing. If you look after us, we'll respect you. We'll never cause you a problem. If anything does kick off, we'll get up and walk out.'

He looked mightily relieved as we made our way to the small bar at the end of the club where Gaffer had been sitting with the girls. Then suddenly we heard – Bang! Whack! Crash! – and three blokes are lying on the deck with Gaffer standing over them shouting, 'I warned you fuckers, stay away.'

The three likely lads had made a move on the girls and

Gaffer had just launched his nuclear deterrent in the shape of three right-handers. I turned to the distraught manager, shrugged my shoulders and said, 'I'm afraid I can't vouch for him ...'

It was typical Gaffer. He didn't bother with small talk. He'd warned the geezers once to lay off the chat-up lines with the girls. He didn't ask twice. With Gaffer, it was one strike and you're out for the count.

We didn't stay for a meal. I'd promised the manager we'd go if there was trouble so we took our spending money to another bar and got stuck into the fillet steaks there and put a nice few quid into their till.

I explained to Matty how important loyalty had been throughout my life and how people like Gaffer were vital to have around you in my kind of business. You took them at face value, warts and all, when you knew you could depend on them.

I told him how so much of the muscle business had centred on Talbot's Gym in Stratford and apart from being heavies for hire, these guys were also my best mates, people you could depend on in a crisis, and I hoped that he'd got friends to lean on when it mattered. The gym, a little place above a shop, was run by Angelito Lester, the British bodybuilding champion and about the best in the business at turning out fantastic physiques. He was tremendous at getting me back into shape after my car crash and got my broken leg back to fitness when I thought I'd be walking with a limp for the rest of my life. Good man, Angie.

Just about every single member of the firm had been

introduced to me amid the sweaty equipment of his gym. Real people, real muscle. No wannabe hard men, no paper tigers, these guys were proud of being tough. With an army of brawn like that behind you, you felt you could take on the world. With the steroids that were readily available on the bodybuilding scene, we'd probably have beaten the world.

For me, the value of unconditional loyalty was never more evident than on the day I had just clocked off from an 18-hour stint at the Ministry of Sound, a couple of fights sorted, a would-be dealer kicked out, and I was sitting down to my first home-cooked meal in a week and looking forward to a day with the kids.

The phone rang. I looked at the clock on the lounge wall. It was 11.05pm. Gotta be trouble. It was. Big trouble. Black Sid and Mad Jack were trapped in the Frog and Nightgown in the Old Kent Road, in South London, surrounded by about 20 geezers who wanted to rip them to bits. We had to bail them out. But they were in deep shit in London and I was in Brentwood 50 miles away. I rang Gary and Kevin in Stratford, which is a lot closer, and told them to get tooled up and get to the Frog and Nightgown and that I'd be right behind them once I'd got myself a shooter and a knife. I rang other members of the firm who were still awake with orders to rescue the beleaguered Sid and Jack.

The team moved like lightning. Gary and Kevin were first on the scene, in with baseball bats. They whacked a few of the opposition, grabbed Sid and Jack, shoved them in their car and headed back towards the safety of East London. We were still on our way, somewhere around Walthamstow, when we met them coming back. A shaken Sid and Jack had had a lucky escape. But they had never doubted for a second that we'd ever turn our backs on them. They knew we'd send the cavalry.

Sid was a bit special in the gang, a big gangly West Indian with one of those booming black London voices like Frank Bruno – 'Ow ya doing, mate, cushtie, cushtie.' You couldn't invent him. I'd taken to him the minute I met him at the gym and groomed him for door work at the clubs. He was a natural, a gentle giant, but with a killer instinct when the chips were down. I can safely say he would die for me and he would kill for me. I hope I never have to prove either, but I know it's true. He's fucked up so many times I've lost count, he's cost me an arm and a leg, but his loyalty has never been in doubt. He's had money, he's spunked it all, but you just can't get the hump with him.

His parents had gone back to Antigua when he was young and he'd been brought up by a foster family on a shitty sink estate in Leytonstone. When the money was rolling in from the rave scene, I asked him one day, 'How would you like to go and see your real mum and dad?'

'What, in Antigua?'

'That's right.'

His face was a picture. I paid his air fare to the West Indies and gave him spending money for a two-week holiday. Whatever stuff I was into, I felt I was giving something good back, balancing the books a bit. To see his joy was worth every penny, two-and-a-half grand well spent. It sealed the bond that already existed between us. A proper soldier to the end.

Now my Sid had been given grief in a South London boozer and revenge was required. Nobody messes with our firm and gets away with it.

That, I told Matty, was the sort of thing our outfit was all about. Loyalty, 24/7. I think he understood.

We hunted down a couple of the ringleaders who'd attacked Sid and Jack and paid them a visit a few days later. I heard they were walking about with some broken fingers and a chiv mark down their faces afterwards. Job done.

Much as I love Sid, I'm glad he's now out of the muscle game. He was such a character, such a party animal, a dreadlocked bird magnet, that he was always going to get hurt or even killed by some jealous rival. He met up with a fantastic girl called Lou, moved from East London to Bracknell in Berkshire, got himself a proper job in the motor trade and now has a lovely baby daughter. Fantastic for a black man from the East End making it in a posh suburb like Bracknell.

And the most marvellous thing is, Sid – or Randolph, to use his real name – has since become a mate of Matty's. He's now given up selling cars and is working for Matty's firm running a gym in Bracknell. It was like it was all meant to be. And, in some respects, it's almost a miracle. I remember all too well how Sid developed a life-threatening lung disease when he was coughing up a cupful of blood a day and needed a seven-hour operation. He had to be flatlined, his metabolism reduced to almost the point of death, for the surgeons to operate. I'd never seen such massive operation scars.

When me and Kevin visited him, we wanted to cry. He

was drifting in and out of consciousness, full of tubes and drips. Then he was with us for a few minutes. He looked as us and said hazily, 'I could see you putting your hand out, Carlton, pulling me, stopping me from going away. You saved me, brother.'

I went cold. The first person I had seen when I came round in hospital after my car crash had been Sid, like a mirage at the bottom of the bed, his big booming voice going, 'All right, Carl, 'ow you doing? Everything OK?'

Had I been there for him when death was calling his name? I'll never know.

15

Raving Mad

J'd never seen so much money. Black bin-bags full of the stuff. Week after week, the rave scene was relieving Britain's youth of millions of pounds of their hard-earned cash and providing me and the boys with the most lucrative minding job we'd ever had. It was the scam of the century, money for old rope.

As I've already said, I was in at the start of it as old warehouses, empty factories, anything with a roof and four walls, even fields beside the M25, were being commandeered for a weekend. Kids flocking in by the thousand. The bow-ties and black jackets were left in the wardrobe as rave party organisers paid us to look cool in jeans and bomber jackets as we helped them pile up the cash from £10–£20-a-time door receipts to sales of soft drinks at rip-off prices. Plus, of course, the rake-off

CARLTON LEACH

from the real earner, the Ecstasy tablets. I thought at first Ecstasy
was harmless, fun and very, very profitable. The old notion of
£50 for a night's work tangling with a load of drunks at a disco
club was out the window. Now we were on £250 a night and
rising. We were on percentages of the profits. We were on bungs
from the E dealers. We were loaded. And we rarely had to lift a
finger in anger as the kids danced the night away to acid house
and strobe lights, full of love and peace for all mankind.

We weren't needed to keep the kids in order, but to keep
the cash intact, make sure some scabby bastards weren't about
to burst in and grab it from us. Organised crime was quick to
take an interest in the rave scene's rich rewards. This was
great stuff; you didn't have to pay for a venue, you didn't
need a licence, you could charge £2 for a bottle of mineral
water that cost 25p and you could summon the kids to the
secret rendezvous through a network of coded phone
messages and pirate radio stations, all the intrigue that had
people fighting to give you money for a piece of the action
like no other fad before.

In 1988, when the bandwagon started rolling, I honestly
thought it was a craze that would fizzle out within a couple of
years and I decided to fill my boots with the easy money while it
lasted. Denny wanted a new car. She's always fancied a snazzy
four-wheel-drive Suzuki jeep. 'Right,' I said one birthday, 'I'm
just popping out to get you a box of chocolates.' She did not
look happy. I drove over to MotorPoint in Romford and
wandered about for 20 minutes looking at cars without anyone
taking much notice. I was in jeans, flying jacket, boots, not the
sort of bloke who might just have £14,000 in notes in a carrier

bag in his motor. I saw the boxer Herbie Hide's old four-wheel-drive automatic with wide wheels and all the biz, but it wasn't ready to go. I needed something I could drive off the forecourt, leave my car and pick it up later. Then I saw the perfect model. A little cracker. 'I'll take that one,' I said.

'How would you like to pay, sir?'

'Cash,' I said.

Well, suddenly I'd got three of them buzzing round me. Take a seat. Cup of coffee, sir? If I'd had a shit, one of them would have wiped my arse. What a difference a wedge of readies made. I handed over the £7,800 asking price, less a little discount for cash, and I drove home in the graphite-grey Suzuki and called out to the kids, 'Where's Mum? You can tell her her birthday present is outside.'

Denny was upstairs. 'What? What's going on?' she said.

'Look out of the window.'

Her face was a picture. A couple of months later, they brought out a new Suzuki Bushwacker jeep, a special edition in black with roll bars, big wheels, running boards, it was my dream motor. So I decided to sell the first motor to a mate and buy the new one. When I arrived at the dealer's this time, they were all over me like a rash.

'How are you, Mr Leach? How nice to see you again.'

'I want to buy the new Bushwacker,' I said.

'Will that be cash?'

Need they have asked? I negotiated an £800 discount for cash then pulled nearly £16,000 out of my bag and stacked it on the desk.

That was the moment I really felt I'd arrived. Bit of muscle, bit of villainy, bit of this, bit of that, the dosh was rolling in. Seemed easy then. But where has it all gone now? One thing I know is that, nowadays, if you went into a car dealer's and dumped £16,000 on the counter, you'd get a tug from the Old Bill pretty quick. In the old days, if you were a face around the East End they'd expect you to have a nice few readies on you and they'd know better than to grass you up.

What the rave scene – or the Ecstasy scene, I suppose, to be more accurate – did do better than any politically-correct sociologists could ever hope to achieve, was to break down barriers, be it race, territory or sexuality. It became as near the global village philosophy as was possible, where people from any part of the world, any colour, with any sexual preference were all genuinely on an identical level. It's a shame it all turned out to be a chemically-induced illusion that eventually claimed so many young lives.

I was in an acid house club called Pushka one night when I got chatting to a black geezer at the bar. It was a night off for me, away from the doors, and I was out to relax and enjoy myself amongst a new crowd of people. I got chatting to the guy and we got on great. We talked about football and music and all sorts. I bought a drink for us, he bought a drink for us.

What I had failed to pick up on was the fact that he was gay. Not that it mattered when it came to just having a beer together. There was a bit of softness there, but I just thought he was just a bit arty, it was that sort of club. He said would I like to meet his girlfriend. Sure I would.

He called her over from one of the tables where she was sitting with a friend. I honestly thought it was Naomi

Campbell, the model. She was beautiful and elegant, and walked like top model.

'This is Celeste,' said my new pal.

'Hello, I'm Carlton,' I said shaking her hand.

'Pleased to meet you,' she said.

Well, the voice wouldn't have been out of place on a building site. She was a he, a transvestite who had managed to convert everything except the growling voice from male to female.

'She's been in magazines,' said my new friend.

I'd twigged that he was on me for more than a beer, that he fancied a bit of bruiser between the sheets. He started squeezing me with his eyes in that way some people have when they are trying to make you like them, all sort of cosy but intense. Well, I started to get a bit paranoid. I realised that all the people around us were gay. I was aware of lots of eyes on me. Did they think I was gay, too, out for a pick-up for the night?

As I've said, someone being gay is not a problem, but now it was getting scary. I was muscled up, tattooed and wearing a vest, so I suppose it was my fault for looking like someone from the Village People. Fortunately, I was with my girlfriend Lynn, but she was sitting at a table on the other side of the room. About half the club were transvestites, and very attractive ones at that, and it was impossible to tell who was who. But I knew I'd become the centre of attraction.

I walked over to Lynn. 'I need a pee, sweetheart,' I told her. 'Will you come with me?'

I was certain that my new friend was about to make a move on me and, frankly, I didn't know how the fuck I would handle it without knocking the bloke out cold and I didn't want to do that. So Carlton Leach, this big hard man, started walking out through the club, which I must say was a blinding place full of interesting, colourful people, clutching the hand of my girlfriend like a naughty boy and wanting to shout out, 'I'm not gay.'

It was a long walk through the club and, by the time we neared the toilets, I had about ten transvestites walking behind me, beside me, all around me, and my bottle was beginning to go. Give me 20 or 30 tough geezers causing a ruck in a club and I'd be in my element sorting it. But this? I was quivering like a jelly.

Then one of the transsexuals grabbed my balls. Well, I didn't know whether to laugh or cry. My first thought was to bang him out. Any self-respecting East End villain would bang him out. Instead, I laughed. I just didn't know what to do. This was a first-time situation and I was lost for words. Then everyone was laughing. It was cool again.

Later on, I got a call from the manager's office and was offered door work there. Pushka had had a few problems, some involving anti-gay people, and they'd been looking for the right security outfit. They reckoned, quite literally, that I'd got the balls for it.

*   *   *

I've never bonded with anyone as well as I did with the pop singer Debbie Harry, from Blondie. She came into the Ministry of Sound one night, between her retirement and her comeback, and though she hadn't been in the limelight much for a while, I recognised her immediately. I had had a right thing for Debbie Harry. Had done for years. I'd got all her records. I was like a big kid. I walked her through the club, got her a table and just had to ask for her autograph. 'It's for my daughter Carly,' I said. Really, it was for me.

Apart from being a big fan of her singing, I admired the fact that she had put her own career on hold to look after her husband Chris when he became ill and could no longer play the guitar.

'How is Chris?' I asked her.

She seemed quite amazed at my concern. She said, 'You know, you are the first person apart from our close family and friends to ask about Chris. Thank you. He's doing OK.'

She got hold of my hand and squeezed it. And she just kept hold of it, like I was a long-lost friend she'd suddenly found again. I was knocked out. Here was I, standing holding the hand of my pin-up idol and talking personal stuff for nearly three-quarters of an hour. I've never been in awe of famous people, and I've met a lot around the clubs, but that night I just melted. When she gave me a kiss and a cuddle as she left, I was over the moon. I was plain old, down-to-earth Carlton the bouncer and she was a popstar, but that night we just connected. It was one of the rare magical moments in the muscle game.

As I was driving home in the early hours of the next morning, I had a mile-wide grin across my face. I thought I'd go in and wake Carly up and say, 'Hey, Carly, I've got Debbie Harry's autograph for you.' Then I thought she probably wouldn't know who Debbie Harry was and, anyway, this is a special one and I think I'll just tuck it away somewhere safe for me. I've still got it.

A lot of people from showbiz like to get to know the doorman at whatever club they go to. Steve McFadden — or screen hard-man Phil Mitchell as TV soap fans will know him — and most of the cast from *EastEnders* are particularly friendly when they are out for the night. I suppose being the sort of show it is and the cast being the sort of people they are, they can identify with the head doorman. After all, I always felt I was playing a leading role in my own special production of *Muscle for Hire* that wouldn't have been amiss in any episode of *EastEnders*.

I was loving it, Mr Big Shot on the club scene, plenty of cash, cars, motorbikes, quality clothes, like half-a-dozen £1,000 suits hanging in the wardrobe that I never wore, a black leather jacket I bought for £1,600 and gave away the next day. I always seemed to be in demand, hob-nobbing with the rich and famous night after night. I thought it would never end. I was happy to treat my whole firm for breakfast each morning after we'd finished at the clubs, or take friends and family out for meals and pay the tab of £500–£600 a time. Then people started taking the piss and ordering champagne at £50 a bottle. People started turning up at my house out of the blue. 'Oh, Carlton, I'm in trouble, can you lend me £3,000? I'll pay it back next week.' Never saw it again. Then someone else wanted money for their kid for something, I can't even remember what it was. I gave them £1,250. Never saw that either. I never really thought about it.

These were friends and I thought they were there for me. They say a fool and his money are soon parted, and I'd become a soft touch for everyone. For example, I'd give a barbecue — free booze, free food, free gear for anyone who wanted it and they'd come in their dozens. We'd maybe party for two days over a weekend. If kids were there, I'd hire bouncy castles and discos to keep them happy.

My parties were a bit like a Mafia convention, or Rottweilers at play. We might have up to 50 great beefcakes from the muscle business there with wives and kids, big hugs and kisses when they arrived and when they left, with the blokes giving me all the shit in between, saying how they loved me, how they would always be loyal to me, how they would kill for me, die for me. They surrounded me, smothered me, told me all the right things I wanted to hear. 'You are the man, Carlton, you are the man. You've got the top firm.' Respect, respect.

You start believing your own publicity, losing touch with reality, really thinking you are some sort of all-powerful Godfather figure. In my mind, I *was* that Godfather with all those people depending on me. But I was living in a goldfish bowl and I couldn't see where I was swimming. I needed to be outside looking in to realise what a phoney world it had become.

The stark reality of that fact was really rammed home when I lost the security contract at the Ministry of Sound in 1992. The bubble burst in spectacular fashion and the easy money dried up. So did most of my so-called friendships, the promises of loyalty as fragile as eggshells. It hit my ego big time. The Ministry was now the top rave venue in London and it was my domain, my kingdom, my whole life and, of course, my main earner.

I was shattered at losing the contract. I was also gutted by the murder of Tony Tucker, Pat and Craig. With Tony's death having been so high-profile, with stories running in the media week after week, I was under the microscope as far as the police were concerned, every move I made was covered, so I couldn't get involved in other work, straight or dodgy, and the cash soon started to evaporate. I was being watched round the clock; I knew I was being watched, so I had to keep my nose very clean. I knew I had to sever all my links with the drug barons who'd paid me so handsomely over the years for allowing them to ply their trade. The death of Leah Betts, and the evocative image of her on her death bed, with her parents' emotional pleas for help in catching the pushers who'd supplied her birthday Ecstasy pills, was preying on my mind. I knew Tony had the door at Raquel's in Basildon where she bought her pills and I knew I was being tarred with the same brush – evil, ruthless, uncaring drug-dealer. I wasn't, believe me, I wasn't. I had no connection with Raquel's, apart from knowing Tony and some of the guys who ran the security there. I did care about the people around me, I did care about the kids in the clubs but I'd got into the Ecstasy scene genuinely believing that this was something for the greater good of mankind, that this was a solution to all the tension, the hatred, the hostility that afflicted mankind. How stupid and naïve, how crass. Once involved I was trapped by the lure of easy money, trapped by the belief that what I did, what I was, was somehow important.

How transparent that all looks now. Where are all those people who had their snouts in the trough year after year, people who were trusted and believed in? They weren't there for Carlton Leach, they were there for what they could get. Will those favours I gave willingly ever be returned? Not a snowball's chance in Hell.

OK, I'm pretty much on my own now, apart from Kelly and a few close friends and family, but I reckon I'm a better person for it. I can now see exactly where I was heading and there were only two routes ... prison or death. When the money was rolling in I was planning ahead big time. I was talking in millions from drugs and violence. I am certain I would have become a truly horrible person, detestable. I think now, with everything that has happened, that I'm a better person. I now hate that flash git I'd become. My close friends, the ones who matter now, have said to me, 'Carlton, you changed for a while and you were not nice at all. We thought we'd lost you for ever, you were so involved.'

What I regret most of all is not thinking about my kids, not making provisions for their future. If I'd got half my brain in gear, I should have been putting all the £800 and £1,000 meals and drinks money into a savings account for the kids to give them a bit of a chance in life. But it was always live for the day, there's plenty more for tomorrow. I was on a roll at the heart of the drugs trade, I was involved in all sorts of villainy and if I needed £500 I could phone up someone, get a bit of graft and earn myself a monkey. When we needed to pay the rent on Lynn's flat I'd pick up the phone, make a call, do a job with someone and earn myself a grand. That's how easy it was. When you are living in that brainwashed environment it's a fantasy land. Nothing is real. Nothing lasts. Most of the people in that world are sheep, there are not many who will stand alone; they'll be in that corner with those particular villains, that champagne, those birds, that Charlie, because that's the corner to be in. Go with the flow while the going's good. It's when the bubble bursts that you realise it's all illusion. Where are the sheep now? They've all got fucking foot-and-mouth disease!

The rave scene has left me with a couple of drugs convictions on my form sheet, along with a bit of violence from the soccer days. I wasn't a dealer, I swear, but I did use Es for the reasons I have explained and I did once get caught in possession of Ecstasy tablets. When we were doing security at the raves, we often popped an E or two to put us in the mood, so we'd be as chilled as everyone else. I used to get them for all the boys, either as freebies from some grateful dealer or I'd buy them at a discount rate.

One night, we were doing security at a riverside warehouse in East London and I'd got 20 or so Es which I intended to give to my personal friends later. But someone had tipped off the police. When we arrived, the whole place was in darkness. I thought that was odd because we knew the organisers would have been in there setting it all up, putting in the lights and speakers and what have you. But it was quiet. I knew something was wrong. But too late.

Before we could turn and make a bolt for it, the police car lights all came on and cops were running from everywhere. I put the packet of pills under my foot. Then a big, hairy-arsed copper was asking us, 'Where you going?'

'We're going to a rave. There's a party at the warehouse.'

The police must have seen we were all lumps, not the average rave scene participants, and we'd got a few tools of the trade with us – a pick-axe handle, a lump of wood, etc.

'Oh, these are from work,' I said, 'I'm a carpenter.'

Oh yeah? Right, get your trousers and pants down, we're going to search you. Let's look in your shoe.

That was it. He felt inside and under my boot and found the Es. I was taken to a police station in North London and questioned for hours. I told the cops that I wasn't dealing and that I'd only bought the drugs for personal use for me and my friends and hadn't intended making a penny on them. The police charged me with possessing Ecstasy with intent to supply. Under the drug laws, if you give someone a tablet, or a piece of hash, or whatever, you are intending to supply. I didn't want to plead guilty to supplying because that would officially make me a drug-dealer on my police record and on my passport. Holidays in America would be out the window. Worst of all I knew it was likely to bring me a prison sentence.

After numerous appearances at magistrates courts, I was committed to the Crown Court and by then had been persuaded that it would be in my best interests to plead guilty to the supply charge. I got slaughtered by the judge. You would think I was the King of Colombia or the boss of some gangland cartel. He looked at me with a face like thunder and said he was remanding me for a month with a view to handing out a custodial sentence. I wasn't scared of doing a bit of porridge, but I wasn't exactly looking forward to it. And while I'd been on bail awaiting trial, I'd been on a curfew so I wasn't able to do any graft to earn a few bob to tide Denny and the kids over if I went down. I was actually living in Brentwood with Denny but giving my mum and dad's address in East Ham. Now I was convicted I had to make sure I stayed at the address I'd given to the court so I wasn't able to be with Denny and the kids, knowing I might soon be going away for a prison stretch. I had to sign on at 10.00am and 6.00pm every day. It drove me mad.

Effectively, I couldn't go out after dark. So on a couple of nights, I got a mate – same size, same shape – to sleep round at mine while I went out clubbing. If the Old Bill checked, they'd be told I was tucked up in bed. If they looked closer, they'd see someone snuggled down under the sheets giving a passable impression of Carlton Leach, right down to the noisy snoring.

It was the longest four weeks of my life. I was certain that I was going away. When the day finally came for me to go and face the judge again, I had a bag packed and had said my goodbyes to a tearful Denny. He asked me again if I was pushing the drugs. I said, 'No.' He made it clear he didn't believe one word. It was like the cell door clanging shut behind me. But one thing had become obvious – the judge had read every single character reference my defence team had supplied. Really read them, not flipped through them in some token gesture.

'Stand up, Mr Leach.'

This was it.

'I am going to sentence you to nine months' imprisonment.'

I heard Denny cry out in the public gallery.

The judge paused, then continued, 'This will be suspended for two years. You will also pay a fine of £500 and £250 towards the court costs.'

That pause was only seconds but it seemed like an eternity. I think that's their way of making you suffer that little bit extra. I was mightily relieved at my narrow escape. The case had come in 1988 before the full impact of the rave scene and the Ecstasy culture was causing concern among the police, public and authorities in general. The pills I'd had were clean, original MDMA, uncontaminated by the greed of organised crime that was to have such devastating consequences in the coming years. Even six months to a year later, I feel I would have gone inside for three of four years. Kids were becoming ill, dying from the effects of Ecstasy and I could have become a scapegoat for the whole culture I had once believed in.

I couldn't believe my good luck in escaping a jail sentence. So it was back to work straight away. The next night, me and Vince got a job from a well-known East End villain to guard a big warehouse full of toys and electrical goods which he thought was going to be broken into by a rival firm. We were tooled up with baseball bats ready for anyone who came through the doors or windows.

The night passed quietly. No sign of any intruders. So I set off home to Brentwood in the early hours looking forward to a nice kip. Four minutes from home – BANG – I had the horrific crash I've mentioned before. I couldn't believe it; in a matter of 48 hours I had escaped a prison sentence by the skin of my teeth and now I was in traction in Harold Wood Hospital with bones sticking out of one of my legs and pain like I could never imagine in seven sorts of hell. Fickle fate or what?

I remember nothing of the crash, it's absolutely blank. Did I fall asleep? I don't know. I hit another car head on but I don't know to this day who was to blame. That was the way my life went. One moment I was counting my blessings, the next I've got a kick in the bollocks as a stark reminder of just how unpredictable life could be.

About a week after the crash, while I was still in hospital police launched their biggest-ever offensive against organised rave parties and drug suppliers. Apparently there had been a 12-month undercover operation at the main meeting point for ravers, Echoes Club in the East End. It was where the scene all came together – the organisers, the illicit radio stations, the venues. the dealers, the DJs, security, everybody. The cops had targeted a number of people they believed were big players. One of them was a Turkish geezer who just happened to look a lot like me. The cops thought it *was* me. They were watching the comings and goings at Echoes, taking undercover pictures and video footage, trying to nail the people they believed were behind the rapidly growing rave scene and increasing criminal links.

So while I was lying injured in hospital, they steamed in for the big raid. They grabbed the Turkish geezer, held him down on the floor, slapped the handcuffs on, roughed him up a bit, then one of the cops said, 'Fuck it, this isn't him, this is not Leach.' They'd been after me because I'd become a well-known face on the scene and they had ended up getting the wrong man. They were livid. Perhaps the crash was a blessing in disguise. After getting away with a suspended on the Ecstasy charge a week earlier, any kind of charge related to raves and drugs would definitely have put me away for a long, long stretch.

It didn't seem much of a blessing as I lay in traction for a total of eight weeks wondering where the fuck I went from there. Muscle man was lying there as helpless as a baby. I saw the bloke who'd been duffed up in the Echoes raid a couple of months later. I said, 'You took a good hiding for me. I'll always owe you one.'

MUSCLE

It had taken the ambulancemen and fire crews two hours to cut me out of the wreckage of my car. It was one of the closest brushes with death I'm ever likely to have. The ambulance guys said an older man, someone without my physique, strength and muscle tissue would not have survived. The impact broke my fibia, there were five other breaks in the same leg and I lost four inches in length which required the broken bones to be stretched back into shape through traction. My nose was broken and needed to be reset. My whole body was black and blue. The seat-belt, said the police, had definitely saved my life. The impact was so violent that the belt had cut through my leather jacket like a knife through butter.

I knew I had a real battle on my hands now. I was weak and vulnerable and people coming to visit me were dishing out pity and saying things like, 'Can't see you coming back from this, Carl.' I was determined I would come back. I really worked at it. Every day I pushed myself to the limit, using a walking frame, making it to the loo and feeling like I'd just conquered Everest the first time I made it on my own, had a shit and wiped my own arse. I wasn't dependent any more. But I had a long way to go.

When the simplest things in life are suddenly taken away from you, when you are in a hospital ward where people are dying from cancer, when the future looks totally bleak, you get a lot of time for reflection. I remember becoming so low, so depressed, I was crying in the early hours of the morning. Then the guy next to me who was receiving cancer treatment was suddenly taken seriously ill. He'd become a friend, we had joked and shared our newspapers. Then one day he was wheeled down to the end of the corridor to die. That was the moment I took a good look at myself and said, 'Carlton Leach, you've just survived a car crash you should have died in. You've got a future, he hasn't.'

I'd been in there four weeks when one of those strange quirks of fate happened that make you wonder what life's all about. A new patient came into the orthopaedic ward. I thought, I know that bloke's face. Then it dawned on me. He'd been the copper at the scene of my crash. Now he was joining me in hospital after being hit by a car himself while he was trying to stop a speeding VW Beetle. It had hit him and roared off, leaving him in agony in the road with a broken leg and broken ankle.

We got chatting in hospital. We were in the same boat now, so we weren't enemies. He told me that the driver of the other car involved in my crash was a millionaire, a Freemason, and had been playing golf with a police superintendent friend before the crash and had then been drinking at the golf club until the early hours. I didn't hear anything more about the accident from Essex Police. I reckon I'd already heard my reason why not!

16

Four Murders
and a Funeral

It was six long months before the police made any real progress in finding Tony's killers as the proverbial 'wall of silence' fell over gangland. It was six months in which I had time to contemplate the magnitude of what had happened in Workhouse Lane, Rettendon, that bleak December night, and absorb the stark realities of what Tony had become. Drug baron, smuggler, killer, addict. A man running out of control on high-octane fuel. As I stood by his marble headstone in Hornchurch Cemetery, I cursed the day that he joined forces with the likes of Pat Tate and Craig Rolfe.

The police breakthrough came on 15 May 1996 when Darren Nichols was taken in for questioning about a consignment of cannabis seized from the back of his Transit van at his home in Braintree. Police intelligence reports suggested he might be able to provide a vital lead into the hit team that had wiped out Tony, Pat and Craig.

Like everyone around the drug scene, I'd heard a dozen names stuck up as the possible killers and I'd heard persistent claims that it was an Old Bill team that had done it. After all, Tony and his firm had made more enemies than friends over the years and the permutations were endless. Even the wildest theories gained credibility.

At that stage, Micky Steele and Jack Whomes weren't on my personal list of suspects. Neither was Darren Nichols, come to that. To me, he was just a bit of low-life scum who floated around at the bottom of the Essex gangland gene pool as the big boys clambered their way to the top. What I didn't know then was that Steele and Whomes were already the prime suspects, but Essex murder squad detectives had been unable to come up with any hard evidence to slap the murder charges on them. The police file was apparently bulging with information about massive drug deals, double-crosses and threats of vengeance, all involving the three dead men and the Steele/Whomes outfit. Customs investigators had been watching all five as well, while speedboat-loads of puff were brought into Britain from Amsterdam via Belgium and the English Channel.

After the murders, Steele and Whomes had apparently returned to normal life with such nonchalance that there were no chinks in their behaviour pattern that would give the cops either positive evidence or cause for suspicion.

That is, until Darren Nichols got his collar felt. Although he appeared on the surface to be a two-bit nobody who dabbled in cannabis, it soon transpired that he was the gangland catalyst whose evidence could be the key to unlocking the Rettendon murder mystery. He'd worked with Tony and his boys, he'd worked with Steele and Whomes. And he knew the lot. He knew about the huge shipments of puff smuggled in from Amsterdam by sea, consignments flown in from Belgium by light plane, he knew the names of drug contacts throughout Britain, he knew who supplied guns to the villains, including a machine-gun sold to Tony and the boys for £300 and, most vital of all, he knew whose fingers were on the triggers the night Tony, Pat and Craig were blown away and their corpses left so mutilated that they could only be identified by their fingerprints.

Nichols had already been tapped up by a maverick undercover copper who suspected he was deeper into gangland activities than his modest lifestyle suggested and had put offers to him about sharing the profits of his illicit activities in return for not nicking him. But from what I heard later, Nichols was having nightmares about what he had seen that night and lived in dread of being the next to be bumped off if Steele and Whomes deemed him to be the weakest link in their murder conspiracy.

Within hours of his arrest, he decided to spill the beans. Word leaked out to the firm that Nichols was about to blow the Essex gangland scene to bits. He started to make statement after statement detailing the criminal enterprises that had made rich men of Tony and his pals, although I don't include myself in that. At that stage, I hadn't got a pot to piss in, though I know I would have been in it up to my neck if the deal Tony thought he was into had come off and he'd given me the 30 grand he said he would.

The police nicked Steele and Whomes and charged them with the triple murders. Nichols was also accused of murder, but knew that, by turning supergrass and giving evidence, he'd get a tupenny-ha'penny sentence and be given a new name and a new life for himself and his family away from the threat of gangland revenge. During the run-up to the trial, underworld contracts were put out to kill Nichols – now the prosecution's key witness, without whom they would have no case – ranging from £100,000 to a quarter of a million. These were threats the cops took seriously. There were a few people I knew who would happily have bumped off Nichols for that sort of cash. But finding him and his family was the problem. The police had him well tucked away in a safe house out of Essex guarded by armed officers and protected by panic buttons, alarms and secret video cameras.

His mum and other family members were followed by villains trying to find out were he was hiding out. Friends were offered money to say where he was. And, apparently, one sharp operator came up with the novel idea of sending a letter to his old address congratulating him on winning a free luxury holiday in Florida in the hope it would draw him out. But the police were monitoring every cough and fart of Nichols 24 hours a day to keep him out of danger.

He finally stepped into the witness box at the Old Bailey in September 1997 to give his version of what he said had happened at Rettendon almost two years earlier. I went along to the court a couple of times but found it really hard to bear.

The picture being painted of Tony as a hard ruthless killer and major drug-dealer who didn't give a shit about anybody was not the Tony I knew. I have to be honest, though, and say that in the six months before his death I had seen glimpses of the monster that drugs had made of him.

I knew that Tony and Craig had probably also been involved in the murder of another drug-dealer, Kevin Whittaker, whose body was found face down in a ditch near the big Ford plant at Dunton, near Basildon, in November 1994. There were no marks of violence on his body but a toxicology report showed that he had cocaine, Ecstasy, lignocaine and ketamin in his bloodstream – and there was enough of each drug to kill him on its own, let alone in this cocktail. But after a police investigation, Whittaker's death was put down to an accidental overdose. The police had looked at the possibility of murder but couldn't find a scrap of evidence. The file was officially closed.

What had really happened, I found out later, was that Tony and Craig thought Whittaker had ripped them off on a drug deal. According to Tony Thompson's very good book on the Rettendon murders, *Bloggs 19*, Tony and Craig captured Whittaker and accused him of stealing a kilo of puff. Tony was supposed to have said, 'Like drugs, do you? Well, then have some more,' and injected him with Special K and cocaine and other stuff as he continued the inquisition. When Whittaker slumped into unconsciousness, he was put into a hire car and driven to Dunton and dragged into a ditch to die. The car, a Vauxhall Corsa, was valeted twice before it went back to the hire company.

I was questioned myself about Whittaker's death but I knew nothing. Even if I had, I don't suppose for a minute I'd have told them because I still believed then that the Tony Tucker I knew was a decent bloke.

The jury in the Rettendon murder trial took five days of deliberations before announcing their verdict – that Micky Steele and Jack Whomes *were* the Essex executioners who'd blown my pal to pieces. Darren Nichols's evidence had been believed, despite the defence team's attempt to paint him as a fantasist, a Walter Mitty who invented his involvement in big-time crime to mask the reality of his real life as a total nonentity.

Steele and Whomes got life. Mr Justice Hidden was scathing as he sentenced them: 'You lured them to a quiet farm track and you executed them. They had crossed your path and you showed them no mercy.'

Darren Nichols vanished off the face of the earth, his birth certificate and marriage licence have been deleted from all files, his passport details have been withdrawn, his insurance number no longer exists.

But what does remain in the Essex underworld is a lingering doubt that the wrong people are in prison for the Range Rover killings and that one day there will be another chapter added to this dreadful episode of murder and mayhem that may throw new light on this notorious crime.

Personally, I want to shut the door on it for ever. I know just how close I came to propping up a headstone myself.

The priorities in my life now are my kids, Carly, Jamie, Jodie and, of course, Matty, and I need to stay around to be there for them when they need me. I worry for them. I know there are dangers round ever corner. I read about pretty girls like Carly falling victim to crimes like date-rape drugging, and I know that all my good intentions about steering clear of violence would be blown to pieces and I'd be out there finding the bastards and ripping their throats out.

I'll always need to exercise the Carlton Leach brand of justice. It's in me. I hope people respect me for it. Carly got to know all about the code of respect in my world of muscle when she was 16 years old. I threw a party for her at the Warehouse disco and all my old pals came along to meet her and wish her well. She was wide-eyed with excitement as she saw the birthday cake with £50 notes stuck in the corners, the dozens of teddy bears in all shapes and sizes, the piles of presents, the champagne corks popping, her first real glimpse inside my world and I wondered if I had been wise. I need not have worried. She's far too smart to set off down that road, to be lured by the empty promises of gangland and the hollow rewards of criminality.

At 19 years of age, she tells me, 'Dad, I know where you have been. You're back now and you will always get love and respect from me and the rest of the family and that's what matters.'

I know she means it. But in my heart I wonder if the day will ever come when I can walk down the street without looking over my shoulder. Or whether the family and my remaining good friends will end up shedding tears over my gravestone when the Devil casts his net.

About the Co-Author

Co-writer Mike Fielder is a best-selling author and former Fleet Street crime reporter. He wrote the highly acclaimed *The Murder of Rachel Nickell* and co-wrote *Gangbuster*, with ex Scotland Yard undercover cop Peter Blexley, which formed the basis of a two-part drama documentary for Channel Four television.

Fielder spent more than 30 years living in Essex and saw first-hand the inexorable rise in criminal activity as villains spilled into the county from their traditional haunts in East London and turned murder and violence into a way of life.